---

imageworks for women

diana mather

imageworks for women

Thorsons
An Imprint of HarperCollins*Publishers*

To my beautiful daughter Léonie, for all her help and encouragement.

To my tireless agent Charlotte, and my partners in Public Image, for all their support.

Thorsons
An Imprint of HarperCollins*Publishers*
77–85 Fulham Palace Road,
Hammersmith, London W6 8JB

1160 Battery Street,
San Francisco, California 94111–1213

Published by Thorsons 1996

10 9 8 7 6 5 4 3 2 1

A catalogue record for this book is available from the British Library

ISBN 0 7225 3205 9

Printed and bound in Great Britain
by Caledonian International Book Manufacturing Ltd, Glasgow

contents

acknowledgements

Peter Wheeler	Broadcaster, partner in Public Image
Charlotte Howard	Fox Howard, my agent
Jane Graham-Maw	Editor at Large, Thorsons
Betsy-Jane Kinsey	A friend
Giles Brandreth	MP
John Fifield	Chairman, Fifield Glyn, Chartered Surveyors
Gerald McGregor	Tack Training Worldwide
Tomasz Starzewski	Couturier
Charles Grimaldi	Director of Corporate Affairs, Rentokil
Midland Holiday Inn Hotel	Manchester
Leslie Spears	Chairman, John Paul Mitchell Systems (UK) Ltd.
Rita Rowe	Joint Managing Director, Mason Williams PR
Vanessa Feltz	Journalist and television presenter
Jennifer Saunders	Actress and writer
Penny Junor	Journalist and broadcaster
James Leith	Writer and man of many talents
Colin McBain	Butler, Burghley House
David Williams	Managing Director, Emerging Markets Search and Selection Ltd.

David Thomas	Head of Development and Training Supply, BT
Hugh Smith	Graduate Entry, BT
Linsey Perry	Graduate Recruitment, BT
Ian Brown	Assistant Managing Director, NWS Bank PLC
George Dearsley	Journalist
Helen Sharman	Astronaut
Louise Leach	Beauty International
Sarah Wetherall	Consultant and partner in Public Image
Delia Corrie	Actress and partner in Public Image
Claire Smith	Television presenter and former Miss UK
Claire King	Actress (*Emmerdale*)
Mary Spillane	Founder, CMB
Leigh Bruce	Head of Corporate Communications, Saloman Bros.
Samantha Thian	A friend
Claire Hill	Senior Lecturer in HRM, Anglia University
Will Whitehorn	Corporate Affairs Director, Virgin Group
Dr John Viney	Chairman, Hiedric and Struggles Ltd.
Dillis Viney	Consultant, Towers Perrin
Lana Jeffers	Managing Director, Middleton Jeffers Recruitment Ltd.
Denise Holloway	Feathers, Tarporley
Rebecca Hooper	Hooper's Shoes
Sue Wheeler	Personnel Officer, Network Productions, BBC North
John Walkley	Organisation and Manpower Development Manager, Royal Insurance
Janet Brown	Graduate Recruitment, Royal Insurance
Baroness Pouget	A friend
Tim Sands (Jamie)	Senior Stylist, New Wave, Altrincham
Dominic	Senior Technician, Harrods Hair and Beauty
Geoff Hackett	Former Senior Producer, Executive Business Channel
Duncan Miller	Lecturer in Media Studies, Redbridge College
Mark Borkowski	Chairman, Mark Borkowski PR
Tara Newley	Singer and presenter on Viva FM
Stephen Jones	Milliner

Sian Richards	Freelance make-up artist and television presenter
Joyce Dean	Senior Make-up Designer, BBC North
Arthur Andersen	Accountants
Natalie Anglesey	Broadcaster and presenter on London Radio
Simon Whittam	Publicist
Leila Potter	Managing Director, Bunbury Domestic and Equestrian Agency
Robin Wood	Chief Executive, Career Movers' Companion
Pamela Holt Model Agency	Model and Casting Agency
Sue Hardy	Guardian Ad Litem
Clifford Merriman	Finance Director, Executive Standby Limited
Jane Bibby	Marketing and design consultant
Jeannie France-Hayhurst	Barrister
Sheena Storah	Physiotherapist
Michele Turney	Managing Editor, Thorsons

introduction

When we meet someone for the first time, ninety per cent of our opinion of that person will be formed within the first twenty to thirty seconds. If we want to project the right image, then, we do not have much time to waste.

We are naturally attracted to people who are similar to ourselves, a bit like an animal recognizing friend or foe by the colour of its fur or the smell of its skin. While we do not usually go round sniffing each other, the subcon-scious mind is very powerful, which is one reason why so much money is spent on research into perfumes and colour. The way someone dresses, speaks, walks and eats all helps us to build a picture of that person. Clothes can tell us a lot about someone's lifestyle, giving pointers to his or her sort of job, salary and background. Disconcerting, isn't it?

There are some people who are either so rich, so successful or so eccentric that the sort of image they project really does not matter, to them or anybody else. Most of us, however, have to take note of the way the world perceives us. So what is 'the right image' and why is it important? We all have an idea of how we project ourselves, but how many of us stand back and analyse the impression we convey to others? First, let me explain why I am qualified to answer these questions.

I am a partner in Public Image, a company that specializes in self-presentation, confidence building, motivation and personal communication, as well as advising on how to deal with the media. Founded twelve years ago, it became well known when cameras were introduced into the House of Commons and MPs approached us to help them improve their image. During those twelve years I have had dealings with hundreds of people from all walks of life. I have worked for organizations both large and small as well as for individuals wanting to 'change their image'.

Before joining Public Image I trained as an actress and singer, gaining invaluable experience in self-expression and voice control. After reading the news for BBC North for nearly ten years, I am now a presenter for the Executive Business Channel. This involves interviewing men and women who might be running their own businesses or have become the chief executives of multinational corporations. This combination of broadcasting and consultancy experience puts me in an ideal position to know what goes into creating and maintaining a positive image.

Is it feasible to create an image? Of course it is, but your image should mirror your personality as much as possible. A drastic change should not be necessary, perhaps just some fine-tuning. A positive image should transmit confidence, competence, reassurance and responsibility. The minute you walk into a room, the effect on the people you meet should be definite. This does not mean wearing power suits with huge shoulder pads, but it does mean dressing with style and care; it means being prepared for any situation because you have done your homework; it means knowing your strengths and weaknesses. Image must be based on reality, so if you know deep down that the position you are going for is not really for you, do not go for it, no matter how tempting! If you are sure in your own mind who you are, what you are good at and where you are going, you will automatically portray a positive image. Let us examine what goes into forming that image.

YOUR CLOTHES

Some of us have a different image for home and work. I am a casual dresser by nature, and am happiest in jeans or leggings coupled with long T-shirts or sweaters, but when I dress up I like to wear something that will get me noticed! I have learned, however, that while this style of dress might have been fine when I was an actress, my current job demands a high standard of classy but discreet dress. I still wear what I like when at home (especially when I am writing) or on holiday, but for work I present a different image.

The right image takes time and thought. Clothes should be set out the night before so that you have time to check for marks or creases, and shoes should be clean. It goes without saying that cleanliness is fundamental. Creating the right image is not just a question of money. The high-street stores provide some really smart clothes at affordable prices. It is, however, a wise plan to save up and buy a few good things that will mix and match rather than lots of cheap items. A smart jacket, a well-cut skirt and trousers and some good shoes will never let you down.

Clothes need to be of better quality as you grow older. If you wear a designer outfit that fits marvellously, you know you look good and 'right', which gives you a huge amount of confidence. The barriers in both career and class terms are breaking down, but there are still certain rules that should be obeyed. Do not worry – all will be revealed as you read on!

YOUR BODY

These days, an important part of a positive image is to appear physically fit and mentally alert, especially in the workplace. The working environment is increasingly competitive, and there is a trend at present for one person to do the work of at least two people. So it is essential to look as though we will be able to stand the strain and cope with the workload. Our personal lives are often just as demanding as we try to fit more and more into what may already be a hectic lifestyle.

Take the thorny issue of weight. A seriously overweight person sends out certain signals. To some, it says 'this person is lazy and probably rather idle'. To others, it might say 'this person is obviously stable and secure in themselves' although, unfortunately, that is less likely. The problem is that you do not know the effect your image is going to have, so it is best to steer a middle course where possible. That does not mean going on a crash diet and changing fundamentally, but polishing up the rough edges.

Not many of us are completely happy with our image, but there are many things we can do to promote a healthy, professional and positive image without necessarily striving for perfection. A nutritious diet and sensible exercise routine is essential to keep us looking good, as is enough sleep; but too often lunch breaks slip by, a bar of chocolate fills that gap and a couple of large glasses of vino help to ease the stress of another long day. Looking pale and pasty does not earn promotion, so in Chapter 1 I will be giving some tips on how to repair the ravages of too little sleep, too much junk food and not enough exercise.

YOUR MIND

A positive image starts the minute you get up in the morning, and it is as much a matter of attitude as anything else. The way you react to other people builds up an image in their mind. Try and think of the effect your actions and reactions will have on others. Show that you care, not only about yourself, but about other people too. We are all human beings living in society together, and life is a compromise. We have to show respect for others, which in turn brings respect for ourselves. If I had a fairy godmother, I would ask her for the ability to communicate well. However strong your message is, it is lost if you cannot get it across. Help is at hand, however, in Chapter 3.

Which newspapers and magazines do you read? It is not easy to converse on every level if you read only the tabloids and *Hello!* magazine. Reading one of the serious broadsheet newspapers at least once a week, as well as magazines such as *Time* or *The Spectator*, keeps you informed of world opinion and events. Nobody expects you to be a political analyst or an expert on the economy, but if you are among a group of people and cannot contribute sensibly to a discussion, it does not do much to enhance a public image!

YOUR VOICE

'It is not what you say, but the way that you say it' that makes people remember and take notice. The way you use your voice is meaningful if you want to make a good impression. Accents are not as significant as they used to be, but they obviously pinpoint where you come from or where you were brought up. We have to be aware that some accents arouse in-built prejudices.

To many southerners, anything that sounds north of Watford immediately evokes the North–South divide. A strong Liverpool or cockney accent could raise doubts about honesty and trustworthiness, and a very plummy accent might be taken as indicating a lack of intelligence and common sense. I am not suggesting that you should necessarily change the way you speak, but it is essential to be aware of the impression you are giving. The most important thing is to be understood wherever you are, and that means speaking clearly and audibly. More on that in Chapter 3.

YOUR FACE

As I have already said, people's first impressions are made on how we look, whether we like it or not, and we ignore that fact at our peril. In these days of equality and political correctness, it is still the case that professional women in management positions who wear make-up get promoted faster than those who do not!

Obviously, ability is what matters most, but if you are representing your organization you must reflect its image. When you stand in front of the mirror what do you see? Most of us are taught that it is vain to spend too much time looking at ourselves, and that self-analysis is only for psychology students. Of course, to spend the day contemplating our navel, or anything else for that matter, would not do us or anyone else any good, but it is important to realize our strengths and weaknesses so that we can 'maximize the positive and minimize the negative'. A smile, for instance, will not only influence how someone reacts to you face to face, but it will also warm your voice when using the telephone.

YOUR HAIR

Hair says a lot about us. It projects an immediate image – the 'dumb blonde', the 'fiery redhead' or the 'passionate brunette'. Those images are stereotypes, but our hair can say whether we are healthy or not and how much we care about our appearance. A good haircut can transform a face and completely alter an image.

STYLE

What makes somebody 'stylish'? Good grooming is essential, of course, but being stylish does not necessarily mean wearing expensive clothes. Rather, it is the overall image of being smartly, appropriately presented in an often understated way. Which women in the public eye do you consider stylish? Thirty years ago, Grace Kelly, Jackie Onassis and Audrey Hepburn, among others, were the epitome of good taste and style; but there are far fewer really stylish dressers today. Women who come immediately to mind are Princess Diana, Joanna Lumley, Rula Lenska and Isabella Rossellini. You might argue that these women can afford to look stylish, but whether you own a fortune or spend one, you cannot buy style. Look at any number of wealthy women in any month in any magazine; they may be expensively dressed, but would you say they had great style? It is easy to be stylish for an evening. Having style means wearing clothes that fit really well; it means wearing something that little bit different (whether it is a pair of shoes, some unusual earrings, a stunning T-shirt or a beautifully cut jacket); it means thinking about yourself and your image; it means taking time.

I suppose it is the sad truth that real style is something we are born with. Think of the people who stand out among your friends. What is it that gets them noticed? In Chapter 2 there are some tips to help you develop your own style.

CONFIDENCE

A lot goes into building an image, and being confident as well as competent is one of the main ingredients. So how can you gain the confidence needed to make an impact and get that job, secure a long-awaited promotion or make friends and influence people? As I said, first of all you have to take a long, hard look at yourself. It can be a painful process as no one likes to admit their shortcomings, but admit them we must if we are going to project the positive image that is a requirement in today's competitive world.

Everybody has positive points on which to build, although it may not be immediately obvious to you what they are. For instance, if you were the eldest child of working parents, and had to look after younger siblings, you most probably have an in-built sense of responsibility that could be valuable for any job in a supervisory capacity. Dealing with cantankerous, ageing relatives also enables you to cope with difficult customers. But how many of you would think of mentioning this on your CV? Holiday jobs and travel experiences are important when it comes to adding up positive achievements and experiences. If you can cook, sew, drive, use a word processor, speak a foreign language, spell correctly or are good with figures, then you can start to build up a list of the things that will help you create a positive image of yourself. It may sound trivial, but everybody has something to offer.

Naturally, academic achievements are meaningful, but for many jobs the employer is looking for something more, so think of something that will give added value and make you stand out from the rest. This need not necessarily be any great feat like running a marathon, but the fact that you can type eighty words a minute, even though the job might not actually require this particular skill, may sway a decision in your favour. Chapter 4 will give you guidance you may be looking for.

SELF-IMAGE

But what is your image? Our idea of ourselves stems from early childhood and from the different events that happen to us as we grow up. Some things have a positive effect, such as a supportive family, doing well at school or excelling in sport. Our ability to communicate with other people also influences our self-image. Other factors in our development can diminish the positive image that most of us are born with. These include the loss of a parent, experiencing abuse, having parents who divorce, moving house a number of times or changing schools.

Whether your self-image be that of a mother, housewife, secretary, salesperson, student, entertainer or professional woman – to name just a few examples – the important thing is to be happy with it. I cannot stress enough that, to succeed in life, we need to have a positive self-image, and in this book I will be concentrating on what we can do to boost it, especially in the workplace. If you feel you have a deep-seated problem, I would advise you to seek help from the specialist books and counselling services available. Once a problem is faced, it is well on the way to being solved.

YOUR SOCIAL IMAGE

People put us into categories when we say what we do. A woman who dresses in a fairly conservative manner and says she is a housewife and mother takes nobody by surprise. If, however, she wears a rather revealing evening gown and dances till dawn, people are surprised when they hear that she stays at home, running a house and three children. It all comes down to our image.

The image we portray socially is often quite different from the one we depict at work. I am sure you can think of teachers who, when you met them after you had left school, seemed totally unlike the people you remembered in the classroom. The image you create in the workplace should stay with you in certain circumstances; if you are 'the Boss' then you cannot afford to let your hair down completely at the office party. But even at other social engagements it is quite possible to tarnish your image. In these days of upward mobility, many people, either through marriage or their job, are swept into sections of society where a particular code of conduct or dress is expected. It is impossible to feel comfortable if you are the only person in a suit when every other woman in the room is in a long, flowing evening gown. It can also be daunting when confronted by an intimidating row of cutlery! Chapter 8 contains tips on social etiquette.

What about public speaking? That is something very few of us look forward to, but when talking to your local film club or hosting a charity fashion show, presenting a positive image on the rostrum is crucial. Chapter 6 will allay all your fears.

YOUR PROFESSIONAL IMAGE

The way you present yourself professionally is the key to success. There are many things that can make you stand out, from what you wear to how you set out your CV, handle an interview or address an audience. Again, the image you create can be negative or positive. The car you drive says a lot about you, but even if you can only afford an old car, it will give you a positive image provided it is clean, well polished and tidy. Shoes and clothes also should be clean and neat, and a well-organized briefcase is important too. And remember that an image has to be maintained once you have taken the trouble to build it up – an image can be broken in the pub, for instance, if drink loosens the tongue. But do not despair. All these things will be looked at in greater detail later.

If you run your own company or manage a department in a large organization, your image should have something in common with that of the majority of people who work there. When the law changed a few years ago to allow the legal profession to advertise, a young solicitor who had just set up a practice rang his local weekly newspaper and asked if they would like to do an interview with him and take his picture in the new office. The paper's initial answer was no. After all, new solicitors' offices open every day all over the country. However, this story was a bit unusual because there was going to be a kissogram girl on the premises. As kissograms were fairly new at the time, the paper sent a journalist round there like a shot! The solicitor got a half-page photo of a girl in lacy underwear and the interview that he had been looking for, saving himself hundreds of pounds in advertising.

That sort of publicity can be a double-edged sword, though. What was the image being projected? Potential clients who needed a solicitor to draft a will for their dying granny might have been put off. Some people, on the other hand, might have been impressed by the flair and imagination of a solicitor blowing away the cobwebs of the legal profession.

How can a company change its image? Rentokil is a recent success story. A decade or so ago, the name Rentokil brought to mind an image of scruffy ratcatchers. That has now changed to one of consistent, high-quality service. Over the last few years, Rentokil has been voted 'UK Company of the Year' and 'Best British Service Company in Europe', among other awards, all of which help to build a positive image, both inside and outside the company.

Rentokil invested their marketing budget in recruitment, training and communication skills, rather than creating the image through advertising. Charles Grimaldi, Director of Corporate Affairs, told me, 'If you work in tatty, scruffy premises and dress as though you do, you are more likely to under-perform than if you dress to a high standard. All those things help to consciously and subconsciously project a positive image.' I chose Rentokil recently to carry out some work at my house. I got several quotes, but Rentokil got the job because the representative turned up on time, wore a suit (even though he had to clamber up into the loft) and had all the relevant information to hand. The other firm I asked to come out and look at my house sent somebody who was wearing a smelly old anorak, gave me some rather dog-eared pieces of paper and did not really seem bothered whether he got the job or not. Added to that, the quotes were similar, so there was no contest!

In Chapter 4 you will find out about careers and what companies are looking for today.

CREATING AN IMAGE

An image is not difficult to create but there always has to be truth and credibility to base it on. If someone is not the sum total of their parts, it will not work. Your image should be a positive thing that will help you succeed, but if it becomes too much of a trademark, it can be a mixed blessing. It happens with actors all the time, but Jennifer Saunders creates so many images for *French and Saunders* that people do not confuse her with 'Edina' in *Absolutely Fabulous*. Jennifer and Edina do not look alike, and Jennifer certainly does not behave in the same fashion away from the set! In Joanna Lumley's case, however, people want her to be 'Patsy', even though their personas are worlds apart.

Jennifer Saunders' image of Patsy when she was writing the part was that of a seedy journalist, someone smaller than herself (although she said that would have meant casting a midget!) and somebody who was not really glamorous. It was a difficult role to cast, and Joanna's name was not even mentioned until Ruby Wax saw her presenting *Wogan* and realized that she was very funny. They sent her the scripts, but it was some time before they could convince her that the image they wanted was not that of the beautiful, sexy Joanna Lumley, but of something rather more bizarre! Joanna has developed the part enormously over the years and Jennifer thinks she has enjoyed creating a completely different image. Now that the series has finished, however, Joanna will have to work hard to lose it.

This is obviously an extreme example, but it is the same for anyone at home or at work. A female accountant is likely to present a more powerful image than that of a housewife, regardless of the personalities of the women involved. It is important to feel proud of yourself whatever you are, and realize your full potential. Whatever we do, our image should be positive. So, if you want to revamp yours, this is the book for you!

CHANGING YOUR IMAGE

Why should you change your image? If you are happy with your current image, there is no need to change it, but there are things about us all that could do with tweaking here and there. Some people, however, need quite a fundamental image change to succeed both at work and socially.

It is often quite a struggle to accomplish a more positive image. I am naturally sloppy and lazy, and never used to take too much notice of what I wore or how I came across to other people. When your children are young it is all too easy to become so engulfed by disturbed nights, nappies and mountains of washing that you have no time or energy to think of anything else. When you do, you can find yourself trapped in a time warp, still projecting the image you had before the children were born. You need to take a good look at yourself to see if you have changed. When I was working as a television newscaster who often had bad news to report, I had to tone down my rather way-out style of clothes, adopting a more sober image altogether. I began to realize that the viewers had a totally different image of me to that of my family and friends. After several comments such as, 'You don't look like you do on TV' or 'You looked really smart in the jacket you had on yesterday' or even 'Your hair looks much nicer when you read the news', I recognized that I had to become much more aware of the consequences of going out looking a complete hag!

Examining things from a different angle, Cherie Blair has also had to alter her image since her husband became leader of the Labour Party. As a highly successful barrister, her uniform was a wig and gown, and her work in court was what mattered. It still does, but facing the cameras as a senior politician's wife means that she is put under a microscope, so she has changed her image quite dramatically. Her hair and clothes are much more flattering now. As she is fairly small, she was swamped by the full-length skirts she used to wear, and the jagged fringe divided her face. With the shorter skirt lengths and her hair swept back, she is able to make the most of her shape and show off her good bone structure.

Chapter 7 looks at these issues in more detail, and examines the implications for your image if your role changes, with you becoming the breadwinner while your partner stays at home, for instance.

MAINTAINING THE IMAGE

Once you have created an image, you have to maintain it, and that is not always as easy as it sounds. Although I now take much more care to get my image right, I have been known to rush out into the car not having completed my make-up, praying for red traffic lights! The following chapters look at ways of creating and maintaining the right image for you, whether it is to improve your chances of getting a job, enable you to make an impression on the social scene or just gain confidence generally. Whatever it is, I can only give you ideas and guidelines – your image must be you!

1

look good, feel good!

To look good you must feel good, so in this chapter we will look at clothes, make-up, skin care, diet and exercise.

CLOTHES AND ACCESSORIES

Clothes are the first thing other people notice about us. You may feel that the clothes I recommend promote rather a 'safe' image. While only you can decide what is the right image for you, there are certain rules for most office-based and managerial jobs, although there are exceptions, especially in the fields of entertainment, arts and leisure. If you follow these guidelines, you will not go far wrong.

In this chapter, I mention just a few of the hundreds of designers and brands on the market, but the biggest tip I can give you is to find a design that you like and stick to it! This does not mean always dressing in the same style – you may like jackets made by Versace and buy trousers at Next. Mondi skirts are a great shape for slim-hipped girls. George Resh produces classic but simple clothes in beautiful fabrics. Kookai is very popular with the young, and suit prices start around £200. Mansfield, Max Mara and Basla make excellent coats that last for ever and can carry you through from morning till night. Jigsaw sell good skirts; Moschino and New Men are good for trousers. Clothes by good designers always look up-to-date, and you can mix and match. The most important thing is that your clothes fit you well and feel comfortable as well as making sure you look great!

Wardrobe Essentials

It is wise to invest in a blazer or a good jacket. Navy is a marvellously versatile colour, and so is cream. Both look classy and expensive and will take you to an interview, to the races, to the theatre and to the office. The jacket must be tailored and smart, so spend as much as you can afford on it. Your next purchase should be a good skirt – one that does not crease, has a classic cut and is knee-length, and therefore always in fashion. Black is probably the most popular colour, as it is so versatile. Good-quality shirts and blouses can be found in high-street shops, so you do not need to spend a lot on these.

A suit is another major investment. Again, it should be as expensive as you can afford. At the time of writing, a suit from Jaeger or Jigsaw will probably set you back about £200–£350. Thomas Starzewski's suits are more individual, in terms of price as well as design, costing around £500–£700. Moschino makes beautiful jackets with rounded lapels. They fit very well, and are always rather different and fun. If you do not want to splash out on a suit, a jacket and skirt by Mondi would be a good buy.

It has to be said that a more structured, tailored suit gives you that edge; and while you do undoubtedly pay for a name, you are also paying for the cut and the comfort it gives, as well as the fabric and the detail. A suit made of poor-quality fabric will show signs of ageing after a couple of years' reasonable wear. Avoid very loose-weave fabrics, as they will pull and lose their shape. Look for a nice firm fabric that will not 'peel'. Betty Barclay is typical of designers who are middle-of-the-road as far as price is concerned; the suits are great but they do not last as long as some because of the quality of the fabric. You get what you pay for, and an average price of £150 gives you a stylish outfit. You can give a good suit a new lease of life by getting alterations made when necessary. Having the shoulders narrowed a little, for instance, can give you a new jacket.

Trouser suits are great for travelling and for wearing in the workplace, where appropriate. You can pay up to £500 for a good one, but you should get five or six years' wear out of it. Trousers are less forgiving than skirts, so shop around, and once you have found a good cut, stick with it!

Try to buy versatile, comfortable clothes that can be worn in different combinations with items you already own. Even Princess Diana wears her clothes for more than one outing. For summer, a fairly fluid skirt with a small print can be very useful. You can wear it with a jacket for work, with a sweater to go to the pub and with espadrilles on holiday. A white evening jacket coupled with trousers or a skirt will do for both a formal or less formal evening. And one decent dress can take you to many different places, so make time to find the right one for you. As well as mixing and matching separates, you can achieve a different look by using accessories. Try adding a scarf or a new belt to an outfit, or replacing the buttons.

Keep the following points in mind:

- Spend as much as you can on jackets and suits, and a coat.
- Choose a good, firm fabric.
- Mix and match clothes in colours that co-ordinate.
- Make sure clothes are comfortable.

Handbags

Handbags need to be practical as well as attractive. They should be made of good leather and, unless you can afford one for every outfit, be of a neutral colour. At the top end of the range, Anya Hindmarch handbags start at about £150 and Gucci bags are priced at around £300. If you can afford it, these are a good buy as you can wear them with anything, they last and they do not go out of fashion. Mulberry make heavier, clumpy bags that hold a lot but would not look so good with a highly tailored suit. Prada bags can be as much as £900, and Chanel are still producing handbags with an immediately recognizable stamp that always says 'quality'. Moschino bags are popular with the young. Retailing at around £190–£300, most of them are not even made of leather, so it just proves there are no hard and fast rules. You do not have to spend that amount, of course, and the high street offers many good alternatives. However, if you make a substantial purchase, you know it will always look good. You can allow a well-designed handbag to look a little worn, but if you buy one in the £40–£70 range, be prepared to change it the minute it starts to look tatty. Look after your handbag by cleaning it with an appropriate leather cleaner, and stuff handbags with paper when not in use to preserve the shape. Do not overfill them, as this will put a strain on buckles and stitching.

The most important points to remember are:

- Ensure the bag is practical as well as beautiful.
- Change it as soon as it begins to wear, unless it is very expensive.
- Keep it tidy inside as well as out!

Shoes

Comfort is vital where shoes are concerned, as tired feet do nothing to improve performance or temper. Russell and Bromley have a good range of shoes in the £70–£170 range. Bally's shoes, which are comfortable and well-made in classic designs, start from around £25. Gabor's elegant, beautifully made shoes cost between £50–£70, and Church's classic designs last for years. Shops such as Cable and Co., Red or Dead and Patrick Cox sell up-to-the-minute fashion shoes at between £40–£100, and high-street stores like Dolcis stock a wide range of styles. There is now a great variety of smaller shoe shops, some of which make the shoes themselves, so if you find a cobbler that suits you, the investment in a hand-made pair of shoes is well worth it.

Once shoes bought at the lower end of the market start to wear, keep them for home use only. Always make sure the heels are not scuffed and keep a pair in the car for driving. It is better to have a couple of pairs of good, comfy, classic shoes than lots of pairs that do not fit properly, in styles that go out of date too fast. It is tempting to go for the latest trend, and that is fine as long as it does not break the bank. If you have a limited budget the safest colours are black, brown and navy, and a really good pair of court shoes and sandals will take you anywhere. Even with a light summer suit you will be safe with dark shoes. If you wear coloured shoes they must be expensive or they will look cheap. Expensive shoes should last longer and do not look tacky when they start to age.

To keep your shoes looking good, always spray them with Scotchguard before you wear them; use shoe trees, wooden if possible; and store them in boxes or on a rack, but not too close together. Keep them clean – use a good leather cleaner, such as Meltonian – and polish regularly. Milk is a good polish for patent leather, as well as the sprays that are on offer from shoe shops. Suede shoes should be brushed with a suede brush to keep them fresh. Never dry wet shoes near heat. If you have splashed through a downpour, stuff your shoes with newspaper and let them dry naturally. That way they will keep their shape and their colour.

The main points to remember are:

- Always buy leather uppers.
- Make sure shoes are comfortable.
- Keep them clean.
- Store them with shoe trees.

Hats and Gloves

Hats are not worn as much as they used to be, but for special occasions they really make an outfit. You can buy hats at any department store from £25 upwards. Hatters like Philip Treacy, Herbert Johnson and Stephen Jones charge anything from £200. If the hat is for a wedding or a day at Ascot it is worth spending money to ensure that you will not see many others like it, but for less auspicious events, you can buy a good one for around £25 to £50.

Gloves should match your outfit. If made of soft leather, preferably kid, look after them well and they will last for years. Store them flat in a drawer. If they get wet let them dry naturally away from direct heat. Long gloves are seldom worn these days except with formal evening wear. Bracelets go over them, but rings go under. You can drink, dance and shake hands with them on, but take them off for eating (or getting married).

Points to remember:

- Storing hats in boxes prolongs their life. Alternatively, stuff them with paper to preserve the shape and store in a carrier bag to keep the dust off.
- Gloves should be stored flat in a drawer or box.
- If they get wet, hats and gloves should be allowed to dry naturally (hats should be stuffed with paper).

Underwear

However smart your clothes are, they will not look really good if your bra does not fit properly. Most women never get accurately measured for a bra, and if they do, they often find they are not the size they think they are! Smaller, specialist lingerie shops offer this service, as do some of the bigger department stores. A good bra will cost around £15 to £40, depending on the material.

Panties, likewise, should fit well. Although they are not as sexy, go for the ones that come up to the waist, covering the bottom completely, or a sexy thong if you prefer more freedom, to avoid visible panty line across the buttocks. Make sure they are not too tight, as nothing looks worse than two hefty lines just below your bottom! There are some good support items obtainable, and tights with built-in panties are another option.

Points to remember:

- Make sure bras fit properly.
- Bras should be thrown away when the elastic becomes slack.
- When wearing trousers, choose pants that cover the bottom.

Caring for Clothes

Do not dry-clean clothes too often, as it is harmful to many fabrics. Hang them outside to get an airing if they smell a bit stale (after a night in a smoky atmosphere for example). Make sure clothes are stored on hangers with enough room to allow them to hang relatively freely. Garments that cannot be washed should have any stains dealt with as soon as possible using the remedies listed below. If the garment has to be dry-cleaned, take care when using shop-bought stain removers as they can affect the dry-cleaning process. If you have used a stain remover unsuccessfully, take it to the dry-cleaners so that they can see what has been applied. Mrs Beaton has some marvellous tips for the care of different fabrics, but you might find it difficult to get hold of all the ingredients – dried fowl's dung and purified bullock's blood are a bit hard to come by these days. Here are a few practical ways to tackle common stains:

- Ink – splash with hot water immediately.
- Red wine – rub with salt or some white wine on a cloth and then wash down with tepid water.
- Grease – dab with eau de Cologne as soon as possible.
- Fruit or vegetable – wash the stain with water immediately, then rub well with Vanish soap before washing.

Jackets are best stored on wooden hangers. Trousers should be pressed and then hung on good, firm hangers, as should shirts and blouses. Natural fabrics need a 'rest', so every so often leave them hanging outside the wardrobe for a day or two. The following tips are taken from a helpful guide called 'Care Information' produced by Jaeger, which is available when purchasing their clothes.

Suede and Leather

Clean garments regularly so that stains and dirt do not get ground in. Use a special brush to clean suede, and wipe leather with a clean, damp cloth. This will also help maintain the even colour of the garment. Do not try to spot clean, otherwise you could leave a mark. Before wearing a suede or leather item, spray it first with Scotchguard or Weather Care. Brush suede jackets every so often to remove surface dirt, then rub with a dry sponge to restore the pile. Should leather or suede get wet, leave it to dry before rubbing the surface with a dry cloth.

Corduroy

Garments made from this hard-wearing cotton fabric can usually be washed. However, to keep trousers in shape it is better to dry-clean them. Corduroy clothes should be ironed inside out on a low setting.

Silk

Silk should be dry-cleaned or hand-washed in luke-warm water using a mild detergent. I hate hand-washing, so I put any delicate garments on the cold rinse–short, slow spin cycle of my machine, and I find it works very well. Colours, however, can run, so if the label says dry-clean, it means it! Do not leave silk to soak for long periods, and never wash silk ties, as they lose their shape. For best results, silk should be ironed while still damp on a medium setting (lower than cotton but higher than wool). Silk needs to breathe so do not store it in polythene bags. Keep it out of direct sunlight, as the colour will be affected. Perfumes and deodorants will affect it too, so allow these to dry before dressing.

Linen

The creased look guarantees linen's authenticity. Some linen is washable and some is not (check the label). Jackets should be dry-cleaned, and linen is best ironed when damp.

Cotton

Most cotton garments can be machine-washed these days, but it is wise to examine the label first. Many shirts and blouses can be tumble-dried too, but again, it is advisable to check. Remove garments from the drier before they are completely dry, and press back into shape. Cotton is best ironed when slightly damp or with a hot steam iron. If you do not have a steam iron, dampen the material with a cloth before ironing.

Knitwear

Good knitwear is usually made of wool or cotton and some is now machine-washable (check the label). Some sweaters have to be dry-cleaned, so check before buying. When machine-washing knitwear, the setting should never be too hot, nor the spin too long or fast, and items are best turned inside out to protect the fibres. Again, to wash anything delicate with 'hand-wash' on the label I use the cold rinse–short, slow spin cycle with a mild liquid detergent, such as Dreft.

When you are hand-washing, make sure that the detergent has thoroughly dissolved in warm water before immersing the garment. Then gently squeeze and agitate it until clean before rinsing once in warm water and then in cold, four or five times until the water runs clear. Always dry wool (or any knitwear) away from direct heat, flat if possible. Cotton pullovers lose their shape easily, so they must be dried flat (on the bed placed on a couple of towels for example.)

If you are using a washing line, fold the garment over so that it will not lose its shape, and peg the sleeves of heavier jumpers. Do not tumble-dry knitwear or hang it over a radiator, as not only could the heat shrink garments, but it will also make the fibres brittle. Iron on a low setting inside out.

Choosing Clothes

Value for money is an important consideration when shopping for new clothes. A well-made jacket should have no puckering where the shoulder meets the sleeve. Its finish is important, and the hems and the buttons should be hand-sewn. Darts and fabric design should line up and the garment must hang well. Test material by squeezing it to ensure that it is not going to crease too much, and if the item of clothing is light in colour, are you going to have to dry-clean it too often?

Body Shape

Another consideration when buying clothes is choosing designs that will do the most for our body shape. We all long for the 'perfect' shape – long legs, a small waist, firm bust, flat tummy – but how many of us actually measure up to the ideal portrayed in magazines? Exercise can greatly help us make the most of what we have got, but however hard we try, we cannot lengthen our legs or shorten our arms. By choosing the right clothes for our shape, however, we can highlight our best points and disguise others. Here are some quick guidelines for the standard female shapes.

Long-waisted, Shorter Legs

Short jackets are the thing here, and belts the same colour as your skirt or trousers to add length to the lower half of the body. If you want to wear a longer jacket, team it with a short skirt that just shows beneath the jacket. If your legs are on the short side, do not wear your skirts too long, as this will emphasize the lack of length. If you have a small waist, make the most of it by wearing waisted dresses accompanied by a striking belt.

Short-waisted with Long Legs

Longer jackets are more flattering as they hide the fact that there is not much length in the body. Short, straight skirts are flattering too, and a belt in the same colour as your top will add length to your torso. Full skirts are a 'no no' for you, unless worn with a long top, but trouser suits look great, as they show off your length of leg.

Pear Shaped

Buy a loose-fitting rather than fitted jacket, as this will help balance your smaller top half. When buying a suit, adding a waistcoat to help pad out the jacket is a good idea, especially if you are a size bigger on the hips. Try wearing a scarf to help keep attention above the waistline. Steer clear of very wide skirts and trousers, and choose vertical patterns.

Triangular

There are more tall, triangular shaped women now than forty years ago. If this is your figure type, make the most of your slim hips and longer legs with straight skirts, which can be either short or long. Pleated skirts look good too.

Jackets should be tailored, but because you already have wide shoulders, make sure shoulder pads are not too big. Dresses hang well on you, but avoid the belted type, as they will draw attention to your lack of waist.

Large

Keep your clothes simple and choose good fabrics. Do not wear anything too tight. Skirts must not pull and buttons should not strain. Loose, flowing, plain-coloured clothes are most flattering. Long, unstructured jackets or shirts, waistcoats and tunic tops look great. Choose good, striking accessories. In her book *Presenting Yourself*, Mary Spillane recommends a scarf or a brightly printed shawl draped over one shoulder. An eye-catching necklace or brooch is another alternative.

Small

Fitted jackets work well on small women, as do trouser suits if you are slim. Avoid long skirts as these will emphasize your lack of height, and do not try to compensate with very high heels. Think tall and you will look taller!

MAKE-UP

I tend to have items of make-up dotted about all over the place. I have a set in the car, a small one for my handbag and a travelling make-up kit as well as the stuff that accumulates in the bathroom or on the dressing table!

However much make-up you have, it is important to keep it in good condition. You do not need to buy the most expensive products, as it is the application that counts. Make sure tops are securely fastened so that nothing dries up, and keep eye and lip pencils sharpened. Wash brushes and sponges after use or they will collect grease and spread it over the face, which can cause spots and blackheads.

Face and Neck

Your face probably gets more scrutiny than any other part of your anatomy, so it has to look good! Good skin comes from eating well, getting enough sleep and taking a reasonable amount of exercise. Being women, we are lucky that we can highlight our best features with make-up and play down the parts with which we are not so happy. We can also alter our appearance to suit our moods, but it takes time and know-how.

Foundation

Foundation acts as a base for the rest of our make-up. Some products also serve to protect the skin from the ravages of weather and pollution. When choosing a foundation, apply a little under your jaw line to ensure the colour blends well with your skin tone. Most department stores have helpful assistants on the make-up counters who can give advice if you need it.

A liquid foundation applied with a sponge tends to give the most natural look. Remember to blend it well into your neck to avoid an obvious line. It is worth buying a good brand, as it will go on smoothly and last that little bit longer without having to be retouched. A foundation from Estée Lauder, Lancôme, Clarins or Guerlain will cost from around £12 to £19, and Rimmel Silk is a very good buy at about £5.99.

Blusher

Blusher is useful to shade or shape the cheekbones and jaw line, as well as giving added colour to pale skins in the winter months. It should be applied just under the cheekbones and extended almost to eye level. A subtle whisk of the brush under the jaw line can help definition. The aim is to look as natural as possible, so blusher should always be used sparingly. If your hair is blonde or grey, pink tints are best. For strawberry blondes, redheads, pale-skinned brunettes, honey-browns and mid-browns, coral and rust shades are more flattering. Olive or black skins need little blusher, or none at all. Bronzing powder applied on the apple of the cheeks gives a natural, healthy look .

Powder

Powder sets the make-up and prevents the skin becoming shiny. Translucent powder gives a sheer, natural look if you do not want added colour. Coat a large, soft brush or puff with powder and apply liberally, pat it in, then brush off the excess. This is not something to do when you are dressed to go out!

Alternatively, you could use compressed powder. Powder compacts range from simple plastic containers to attractive accessories. However you carry it, compressed powder should be a shade lighter than your foundation and in peak condition, so make sure it does not get damp or greasy. It is also a good idea to use a cotton-padded puff instead of the thin, foam pads that are packaged with compressed powder.

You can now buy 'two-in-one' foundation and powder. Some are better than others. Dior's 'Tient Poudre Dual Powder Foundation' retails at about £23, but there are cheaper options from Max Factor and Kanebo from £6.99. Kanebo's 'Total Finish' is particularly good because you can use it as powder with a brush, or as foundation with a sponge. Bear in mind, however, that some of these products are quite heavy, and can dry to a cake-like texture which shows up every line.

Concealer

To conceal the odd pimple or hide any bags under the eyes, 'Touche Éclat' by Yves Saint Laurent is a liquid concealer in a wand. Suitable for all skin types, it lasts for ages and sells at around £17. 'Cover Girl Invisible Concealer' costs about £4. Vincent Longo concealer is also good for covering dark shadows as it does not seep into lines around the eyes. At £6.50 it is good value. Mail order is available on 0171-491 4401. Estée Lauder's 'Disappear' blends easily into the skin and costs around £13.50.

If you are feeling tired or under the weather, your skin might need a good pick-me-up. There are several on the market at a range of prices. Clarins' 'Beauty Flash Balm' (£18), Lancôme's 'Vivéclat Mask' (£18.50) and 'Brighten Up, Tighten Up' by Ultima 11 (£16) smooth tiny lines and give a healthy glow to the most jaded skin. Dior's 'Basic Tient' in Pure White (£19) and 'Translucent Make-up Base' by No. 7 (£5.75) tighten and even out the skin for a quick lift. To reduce puffiness around the eyes, try Clarins' 'Skin-Smoothing Eye Mask' (£18) or Estée Lauder's individually wrapped 'Stress Relief Eye Masks' (£19.50). If you really want to splash out there is 'Issima Midnight Secret' by Guerlain (£64).

Self-tanning Lotions

If you have clear, pale skin and do not want to wear foundation, a self-tanning lotion might be the answer. 'Auto Bronzante' by Clarins and Estée Lauder's 'Self-Action Tanning Lotion' are excellent and priced around £15. It is better to spend a little more on these products as the more expensive ones do not have that tell-tale smell. They last about four to five days before you have to top them up, and your skin will not turn orange as long as you do not put too much on. It is important to blend the lotion in well, so that it dries smoothly. For the best results, it is a good idea to exfoliate and moisturize the skin first. Ambre Solaire's 'DuoTan Self Tanning Leg Bronzer' spray is perfect if you want to go without tights or stockings before you have had a chance to get into the sun. Bronzing powder is also good for topping up a tan, but avoid the shiny ones as they just make you look hot and sweaty! Self-tanning lotions and make-up starts at around £5.99.

Black Skin

If you have black skin, you probably need very little make-up, but there is much more on the market these days if you want to wear it. Brands include Flori Roberts, Bobby Brown and Leichener's 'Blend Of Coffee'. Remember to blend foundation well into the neck. Black skins tend to be slightly oily (which means they age better) so it is important to finish with either a truly translucent or dark powder. You can use powder on its own if you want a matte finish.

Make-up tips to remember:

- Use foundation to give a smooth finish to the face.
- Apply powder to damp down the shine.
- Keep make-up in good condition.
- Clean brushes, powder puffs and sponges regularly.
- If in doubt, have a make-up demonstration to find out what suits you.

Eyes

Eyes are said to be the windows of the soul, so make the most of them.

Eyeliner

Eyeliner can enhance the size and shape of the eyes, but it should be worn sparingly. Guerlain have a new liquid liner on the market priced at around £15. To apply pencil or liquid eyeliner to the upper lid, pull the skin at the outside of the eye very gently until the eyelid is straight. Apply a thin line from the outer edge of the eye, ending in the middle. This enhances the eye without giving the hard 1960s look. The line on the lower lid should also start at the outside and end in the middle of the eye. Use your fingertip or a cotton bud to blend it in so that it looks natural. Use black eyeliner if you have brown eyes or thick black lashes. Grey or brown is a better colour for pale skins and lighter eyes. If you use a kohl pencil, remember than it can 'bleed' causing a build-up in the corner of the eye, so do check your eyes intermittently.

Eye Shadow

Eye shadows come in all the colours of the rainbow, and more besides. You can choose from creams, powders and pencils. Personal preference is what counts, but it is as well to be aware of one or two things.

Pencils should be very soft so that they do not pull the delicate skin around the eyes. Although they are very handy as they do not take up much space, they can leave a rather harsh line, and the colour sometimes sinks into the creases of the eye. Pearlized or satin finishes also have a tendency to crease and accentuate any lines. Use a cotton bud to blend the eye shadow once it is applied, and avoid colours that detract from the eye's natural hue. Princess Diana used to wear a bright-blue eyeliner which made her own blue eyes look much paler, so look in the mirror to see how much depth of colour there is in your eyes.

Boots, Body Shop, Marks and Spencer and Sainsbury, along with all the major cosmetic houses, produce a marvellous range of colour combinations in pallets of various sizes. These are priced from £2.99 to £16.

Here are some guidelines for choosing the colours to suit you:

- Brown or black eyes require beige, copper, taupe, ochre, brown, deep purple, sage green and charcoal. Matte colours are better for black skins.
- Blue or grey eyes need primrose, pale coral, apricot, taupe or plum. To add emphasis and to complement brightly coloured clothes, try lilac, violet and lavender. Beige and mid-brown give depth in the socket line.
- Green and hazel eyes are enhanced by tints of aubergine, oyster, primrose, ochre, beige, apricot, cream and light brown.

Mascara

A good mascara is essential. I have tried most brands at various prices, ranging from £1.99 to £15, and I would not necessarily say that the most expensive is the best. Mid-priced brands, like Yardley or Max Factor's 3000 at £3.99, last just as long as some designer names, so it is a matter of finding the one that suits you.

You can now buy many different types of mascara, from those with added conditioners and lash-lengtheners to ones that will wash off easily. If you are troubled with allergies, hypoallergenic products are available from

Clarins, Clinique and the Simple range. If your eyes tend to run a bit when you laugh, a waterproof mascara could be just what you need; good products are available from Lancôme and Max Factor.

Black is the most popular colour choice for mascara, but for paler eyes, especially green or hazel, brown is a softer option. If you have grey or blue eyes, a dark navy might make a nice change. Having the eyelashes dyed is a useful option for fair-haired people with very pale lashes. It lasts about a month and costs around £10. There are some home dye kits on the market, such as 'Dyelash' by Original Editions, but if you are going to do it yourself, make sure you are not in a hurry, and do not try it just before an important date! It is good to ring the changes, so try some different colours once you have established that you can tolerate the brand.

Eyebrows

Eyebrows need to be tidy but do not pluck them too drastically as they will cease to grow after a certain time. If they need definition, apply matte eyeshadow with a brush as it gives a softer line than a pencil. Use a colour similar to that of your eyebrows.

Eye make-up points to remember:

- Avoid colours that detract from your own eyes.
- Blend eyeshadow in well to avoid harsh lines.
- Use a brush rather than a pencil for eyebrows.

Lips

A good lip pencil is essential to trace the outline of your lips and enhance your mouth. It also acts as a good base coat worn under lipstick. Your lipstick should complement the colours you are wearing and match your blusher. For blonde and grey hair, pinks and pinky-brown shades are lovely (only wear bright red if you are out to make an impact; do not forget that red spells danger!). Brunettes look especially good wearing bluey-red, orangy-red and dusky pink, while redheads look stunning with brown, coral and dusky pink shades, or just plain lip gloss.

Sian Richards is a make-up artist and presenter on BBC's *Good Morning*. She gave me a very useful tip – try satin eyeshadow on your lips under lip gloss for a very subtle, natural colour. Here are some other points to remember:

- Use a lip pencil to define the lips.
- Lipstick should match your blusher.
- Be aware of the effects of wearing very bright lipstick.

SKIN CARE

We all aim for healthy, glowing skin. Diet plays a very important part in skin care (*see 'Diet', pages 24 – 5 for more information*), and deep sleep is essential for the body to renew itself. While we are asleep, our cells divide at a much faster rate and a growth hormone is released into the bloodstream causing regeneration. Some people can function on four or five hours' sleep a night, while others need nine or ten. Whether you need little or lots of sleep, always listen to your body when it tells you it is tired.

Looking after your skin from the outside is also essential. There are countless skin-care products available, and prices range from about £3.99 for the Simple range to £90 for La Prairie. A dermatologist friend of mine once told me that a wipe with a damp sponge is all skin needs to keep it clean. While this may be the case for people who do not wear make-up, travel on tube trains or shop in polluted cities, most of us need to work a little harder on our skin-care routine. Pollution levels are so much higher than they used to be that the skin is subjected to far more harmful chemicals these days, and the thinning of the ozone layer also has a significant effect.

Cleansing, Toning and Moisturizing

Protecting and cleansing are the order of the day. It is advisable to wear a moisturizer with UVA and UVB screens all the year round, as it will help guard against everyday contamination as well as harmful rays. 'Fluide Multi-Confort Super Hydratant' by Clarins protects against pollutants, air conditioning and daylight. It can be worn alone or over a day cream. If it is very hot and sunny, use a facial sunscreen. Brands include Ambre Solaire and E45, and prices range from £5.99 to £15. E45 is also a very good, inexpensive night cream.

Lanolin has earned a bad name for allergies, but in many cases it is the product containing the lanolin that causes the problem, rather than the lanolin itself. If you can use lanolin, it is a marvellous barrier as it holds moisture in the epidermis while keeping dirt and pollutants out.

Every night and morning, you should cleanse the face and neck thoroughly with a lotion or a cream. Remove the cleanser with cotton wool, using an upward motion. If you prefer to wash your face, you can choose from a range of facial washes and cleansing bars. Liquid gels are also available, which are more gentle. If you do not want to spend too much on a cleanser, Pond's Cold Cream costs around £3.50.

After you have cleansed, it is advisable to use a toner. I usually get witch hazel and rose-water made up at the chemist for about £1.99. Follow this with a good night cream. Clarins, Estée Lauder, Elizabeth Arden, Lancôme, La Prairie or any of the other cosmetic houses will provide you with what you need at prices starting from £7.99. Any department store or beauty salon will be happy to give you advice on which skin-care products are right for you. Again, I think I have tried nearly everything on the market – my philosophy is to change the brand every two or three months, and it seems to work! On the other hand, if you find products that suit you, then stick with them.

If you have problem skin, products are available to suit you. The Sher System, 30 New Bond Street, London W1Y 9HD, operates a complete mail-order service for their gentle, water-based skin-care regime. Their make-up gives a very natural look. Products range from £9 to £35. They also provide skin-care and make-up consultations for clients, especially those suffering from acne, hypersensitive skin and rosacea.

Facial

A facial usually begins with a massage lasting for fifteen to twenty minutes. Your skin is then thoroughly cleansed and a face mask is applied. Having a facial benefits the skin by stimulating and refreshing the facial muscles as well as encouraging the blood supply to the surface of the skin. It is also a marvellously relaxing experience. If it was enjoyed by everyone at least once a month I am sure it could replace valium as a stress-reliever. Aromatherapy is very popular these days, and beauticians often use essential oils in facial treatments. Please ensure your beautician is fully qualified, as essential oils can have powerful effects and must be used responsibly. If you are tempted to use aromatherapy at home, make sure you have a good reference book to hand (*see 'Bibliography', page 151*).

Body Care

Do not forget to look after the skin on the rest of your body. Hands, elbows and knees age us more accurately than any other part of us. Hands should be kept well moisturized, and it is a good idea to wear sunscreen on them every day as soon as it gets warm, especially in the car, as the sun shining through the windscreen can become quite intense. Use a body lotion like Revlon's 'Dry Skin Relief' or Vaseline 'Intensive Care' with UVA and UVB protectors.

After the age of thirty, the skin begins to dry up. Keep skin nourished by adding a few drops of olive oil to your bath water from time to time. For a really relaxing soak, try diluting a few drops of essential oil in an egg cup-full of olive, almond or wheatgerm oil and adding to your bath (but remember to clean the bath well afterwards to avoid slipping!). Use a loofah to remove dry skin. When you get out of the bath, massage yourself with body lotion while the skin is still warm and damp for greater absorption. I also massage cream into my knees and elbows every night and morning to keep them supple.

If you are going without tights or stockings in the summer, make sure your legs are waxed regularly. Moisturize your legs every day, especially if you have black skin, as it adds a beautiful sheen. In the sunny weather, a sun cream makes an ideal body lotion, whether you are going to sunbathe or not.

Tips for beautiful skin:

- Always wear a protective moisturizer.
- Cleanse the skin at night and again in the morning.
- Use a good night cream.
- Keep hand cream by the sink to use regularly.
- Use oil in the bath from time to time.
- Do not forget to moisturize legs, knees, elbows and neck.

GLASSES

The wrong shape of glasses can spoil the prettiest face. However much you may like a particular style, do make sure it suits you before you buy what can be an expensive item. The top of the spectacles should be in line with your eyebrows, and the bottom should be no lower than the top of your cheekbones. If in doubt, ask your optician for advice.

Eyes should be checked regularly, as they are an early-warning system for a number of ailments, including glaucoma and high blood pressure. If you wear contact lenses, make sure you keep them really clean or they can cause permanent damage to the eyes.

TEETH

It is very difficult to have a sparkling smile if your teeth are crooked or dingy. The world of cosmetic dentistry has produced marvels over the last few years, but with more and more dentists going into private practice, the cost of getting your teeth done is growing. There are several insurance plans available, which may be worth your investment if you think you may need work in the future. If your teeth do not fit your mouth properly it is impossible to speak clearly, but it is never too late to visit an orthodontist. Caps, crowns, bridges and veneers can transform your face, never mind your mouth.

It is wise to have a check-up at least twice a year, and to visit the hygienist every four months for a clean and polish. Cleaning teeth regularly is part of everybody's routine, but it is important to use dental floss and a good brush. Tea, coffee, red wine and tobacco can stain the teeth, so use a stain-removing toothpaste or a tooth-whitener such as 'Pearl Drops' every now and then.

HAIR

Your hair should be your crowning glory, but a poor diet, smoking, medication and too many late nights can all contribute to poor hair condition. A good diet is fundamental (*see 'Diet', pages 24 – 5*), as is a good haircut that shows your face to best advantage. This will cost you anything from £20 to £70 depending on the stylist and salon, and will last six to eight weeks before it starts to look out of shape.

Finding a Stylist

Choosing a hairdresser is as much down to personal chemistry as anything else – provided that he or she is competent. The image of the staff and the appearance of the clients will help you get an idea of the sort of stylists that work there. If, for example, the clothes are extreme, the cuts are likely to be adventurous too. I went into a new hair salon recently and was slightly confused when asked if I wanted 'an artistic director'. When I looked blank, the receptionist asked if I wanted a 'senior stylist'. That was exactly what I wanted – preferably without the delusions of grandeur!

The busiest stylists are not always the best. A newly qualified hairdresser can be just as good, so ask around and look at your friends, especially the ones who have similar hair and colouring. A satisfied customer can only be a good advertisement. When you have found a stylist you trust, who listens to what you want and cuts your hair in a style that suits you, stay with him or her!

Choosing a Style

If you have a good idea of the style you want, try and find a picture to take with you to the salon. Alternatively, if you have no idea, ask to look through some magazines for inspiration when you arrive. It is important, however, to listen to the advice of your stylist. If the style you long for will not suit you, he or she will explain this to you and suggest something more appropriate. Give your stylist a chance to get to know you and your hair. Any reasonable salon is happy to reappraise a cut if you do not like it or to put more highlights in if you have not achieved the sun-kissed look you were aiming for. But you cannot expect them to be so willing if you have flatly gone against their advice.

Shampoo and Conditioner

Keeping hair in good condition also requires a good shampoo, especially if you wash it every day. Most shampoos are detergent-based, which means they are alkaline and cheaper to make, but harsher for the hair. 'Two-in-one' shampoo and conditioners are useful if you are in a hurry, but they do not really nourish the hair. They are also alkaline, and the gloss they give comes from silicone in the conditioner. Most hairdressers do not recommend them.

Shampoos like Nutra-clenz 'Nucleic A' or those produced by KMS, Paul Mitchell and Redken are acid-based, which matches the natural pH-balance of the hair. They are more expensive but it is worth paying extra, and that goes for conditioners too. Do not expect instant results, however, as it will take a month or six weeks to see the real benefits.

There are several anti-dandruff shampoos on the market, including those produced by KMS and the Svenson Hair Clinic, which specializes in scalp problems. Baby shampoo is very pure, and is good to use for a time if the scalp is very sensitive. Washing hair with cool water can also help.

Hair Care

Brushing helps the scalp as it removes any dry skin, and massaging the scalp encourages hair growth. Hairbrushes and combs should be cleaned regularly. To avoid splitting the hair, always use a brush which has bristles with rounded ends.

Hair obviously needs to be kept clean, but too much washing and brushing can stimulate the glands, making them produce more oil. Half an egg cup of lemon juice dissolved in a jug of water will help remove excess oil from the hair, and an egg cup of cider vinegar in rinsing water can help restore the pH-balance if you have been using alkaline-based shampoos and 'leave-in' conditioners for a long time.

Hair Styling

Do not use a very hot dryer on your hair, as this can be damaging. It is best to leave hair to dry for a while before blowing it, as it gives it more body. If, like me, you have medium-to-long, fine hair, it is a good idea to put your head down and blow-dry the hair from underneath. This not only adds volume, but also allows freshly oxygenated blood to feed the face and scalp. A blow-dryer lotion or mousse will help give hair extra lift.

If you are working in an office or hold a senior position, long hair lacks credibility unless it is put up or tied back. If you cannot make time to visit the hairdresser before an important event, trying a different style might tide you over. Gelling hair to make it smooth and putting it up might hide unruly layers and split ends.

Coloured Hair

Coloured hair must be retouched at the roots as soon as regrowth appears. Hair-colouring technology has advanced dramatically over the last few years. Ask your hairdresser which is the right preparation for you. There are hundreds of home hair-colouring kits on the market. These range from the shampoo-in variety that wash out after a few weeks, such as 'Harmony', to the more permanent types made by companies like Wella and Schwarzkopf. You can buy them from as little as £4.99. Highlights or lowlights should be done by the professionals as, for the effect to look as natural as possible, a very experienced hand is needed. I would always recommend the tin-foil method rather than the cap, as it enables the colour to get nearer the roots. The cost ranges from £15 for the cap method to £80 for foil. Sun plays havoc with colour, so if you really want yours to last, wear a hat – it will protect your face too.

Perms

Perms come in and out of fashion, and are another option if you want to change your image. Again, you can buy home kits to curl or straighten your hair from as little as £4.99, whereas going to a salon will set you back anything from £10 to £70. On the whole, however, a salon perm is money well spent.

Keep these points in mind if you want your crowning glory to be just that:

- Find a good hairdresser!
- Eat a well-balanced diet.
- Choose a hairstyle that suits your type of hair.
- Get a good haircut.
- Use an acid-based shampoo and conditioner.
- Protect coloured or bleached hair from the sun.
- Keep hair tied back in the office.

NAILS

Nails must always be clean, whether they are long or short, and polish should never be chipped. I knew of a company that lost a big training contract because the representative had chipped nail polish. The competition was so fierce that something as small as that was the deciding factor. The fact that the representative had not taken the time or trouble to revarnish her nails raised doubts as to commitment, and did not create the positive image that was needed.

If I want to feel really good I go for a manicure. It gives me great confidence to have my nails looking smart, probably because they are naturally so awful! If I have a number of important meetings, filming days or seminars, I invest in acrylic false nails that instantly give me the nails I long for. False nails are very useful if you have trouble growing your own, but they do weaken the nails when you have them taken off and they need quite a lot of attention. Layers of acrylic are painted onto the nails, which are then sealed and polished. If done well, they look very effective and completely natural. Fibreglass extensions are more hard-wearing as they are made from fine strips of fibreglass which are buffed, sealed and polished. They also look good, but they are thicker than acrylic tips. The cost is roughly the same, between £30 to £40, and the nails will last for months if properly looked after. As the nail grows, the extensions have to be filled from the base every couple of weeks at a charge of about £15. There are also some good nail-strengthening products and treatments available. Sally Hansen's 'Hard As Nails With Nylon', 'Glossy Glaze' from Eylure and 'Formula B' by Nailtiques are priced from around £3.99.

Nails should never be too long. Apart from being impractical, they are rather frivolous and send out the wrong signals, as does very bright polish. One school of thought says that if you spend that much time on your nails you will not have time for much else – it seems we cannot win! Seriously though, if you are doing your job well it does not matter how bright your nail polish is, but when meeting someone for the first time, be aware of the image you are projecting. To play safe, stick to clear or pastel shades that match your clothes. French-style manicures are very popular at the moment and look natural but stylish. The tips of the nails are coated in white varnish, then the whole nail is covered with a flesh tone.

Do not forget your toes! Toenails are not the most attractive part of our anatomy, so keep them well scrubbed. If you go without shoes in the summer, use a pumice stone to keep heels and soles smooth. Keep your feet in good order by treating yourself to a pedicure every so often, and visit the chiropodist if there is a hint of a corn. I think a coat of polish does wonders too, but chipped nail polish is just as unsightly on toes as it is on fingers. Reapply polish when you are not about to put your shoes on, such as when you are watching television in the evening.

For nails to be proud of:

- Keep nails spotlessly clean.
- Manicure regularly.
- Keep them reasonably short.
- Make sure polish is not chipped.
- Do not forget those toes.

DIET

To look good, feel good and create a positive image, we need to eat foods that replenish cells quickly, provide energy and give us pleasure too. Skin, nails and hair suffer if our diet is not well balanced, and low energy levels can affect confidence in both professional and personal life.

There is enormous pressure on women to be slim. For many of us, however, it is not what nature intended, so look at your body realistically and ask yourself how easy it is going to be to achieve the shape and weight you want. Although it is important not to fight too hard against nature, a good diet and regular exercise are essential elements of a healthy lifestyle. A diet high in fat, sugar and processed foods and low in fibre is clearly hazardous to health. If you are a 'picker' you can consume a large amount of food without even realizing it. As a test, write down every mouthful of food that you eat during the course of one day; you may well be horrified by how much it can amount to. If you are an enthusiastic cook who tastes the food as you go along, try an experiment. For every spoonful you taste, put one in a bowl. Some people find they have eaten a meal before they have even finished cooking! Moderation in all things is the key to stress-free dieting.

I do not have to tell you how many different diets there are on the market. I have been on so many diets over the years that I could write a book on them. Like many women, I have dieted even though I am not overweight. I have finally come to terms with the fact that I am just not the shape I want to be, and I do not diet any longer. If I want to lose a few pounds, I cut out all junk food, drink plenty of water and eat smaller portions, making sure I chew the food properly. It really can be as simple as that. Cutting down on fatty foods and eating fruit instead of crisps or snack bars will also help. It is a good idea to have two or three alcohol-free days a week. Drinking water helps clear the system of toxins, and moreover fills a hunger gap between meals. Our thirst 'pangs', which decrease as we get older, are often mistaken for hunger pangs. If you are feeling tired or develop a mild headache, it can be a sign of dehydration, and a glass of water will often put you right. A litre a day is the minimum everyone should drink, and it is better uncarbonated. If you do not find the thought particularly palatable, try adding a few slices of lemon, orange or mint to a jug of water and leaving it in the fridge overnight.

Key points for a healthy diet and well-tuned body:

- Drink at least a litre of water a day.
- Eat as much fresh food as you can.
- Cut out junk food and sugary or fizzy drinks.
- Choose fish rather than too much red meat.
- Limit your intake of fat.
- Keep tea, coffee and alcohol consumption to a minimum.
- Eat dairy products sparingly.
- Make sure you eat a balanced diet of protein, carbohydrate and fresh, raw fruit and vegetables every day (eat as many raw vegetables as you can, but do not eat too much fruit – our ancestors only ate it in season, and too much acid can cause spots).
- Remember – most things are all right in moderation!

Detox Your System

If you want to give your system a pick-me-up and lose a couple of pounds into the bargain, you might like to try an occasional 'detoxing' day, during which you eat only fruit and drink as much water as you can. As an alternative to fruit, brown rice mixed with vegetables is a good purifier too. Choose a day when you are unlikely to be running a hectic schedule or under too much stress.

Vitamins and Mineral Supplements

I take vitamin and mineral supplements in the winter, or if I am working particularly hard. I believe they keep me fairly free of colds, as well as improving my skin, nails and hair. Do not expect instant benefits, however, as it takes two or three months to notice the difference. Your local health-food shop can give you advice on which supplements are right for you. Some supplements can be dangerous if taken in too high a dosage, so always read the instructions carefully, and consult your doctor if you have any doubts. For further information on nutritional supplements, see *Thorsons Complete Guide to Vitamins and Minerals* (Thorsons, 1989).

COMPLEMENTARY THERAPIES

There is a growing interest in complementary therapies, so called because they are intended to be used alongside conventional medicine, although for many ailments they can provide an effective treatment on their own. Complementary therapies are perceived as more gentle than conventional medicine as they tend not to be associated with as many side-effects, and some therapies, such as massage and aromatherapy, are very pleasant to receive.

Homoeopathy

Homoeopathy is based on the principle 'like cures like'. A homoeopathic remedy that produces particular symptoms in a healthy person will be used to cure the same symptoms in an ill person. Although homoeopathy can be a good alternative to prescribed drugs, you should always consult your doctor first if you feel you have a problem.

To find a qualified homoeopath in your area, contact the British Homoeopathic Association, 27a Devonshire Street, London W1N 1RJ or the Society of Homoeopaths, 2 Artizan Road, Northampton NN1 4HU. If you want to find out more about homoeopathy, there are now many books available, and the main commercial suppliers of homoeopathic remedies, Nelsons and Weleda, produce easy-to-read booklets which are available from health-food shops and many pharmacies. Here are just a few of the myriad remedies on offer (the normal dosage is two tablets taken every hour for six doses, then three times daily until better):

- Aconite 6 – treats colds and flu; also has a calming influence, so is useful to take before an interview, for example.
- Arnica 6 – marvellous rubbed on bruises or strains; can be taken orally if you are mentally or physically tired.
- Arsen. Alb. 6 – helps cure food poisoning, vomiting and a very runny cold. It is important to remember that sickness and diarrhoea are nature's way of cleansing the system, but if symptoms persist, see your doctor.
- Gelsemium 6 – useful for flu and real apprehension, such as exam nerves.
- Hamemmelis – very good for keeping varicose veins at bay.
- Nux vomica – an indigestion remedy. It helps with hangovers too!
- Rhus. tox. 6 – very good for rheumatic pain and strain after a long day in the garden or a lot of physical exercise.

Herbal Remedies

Herbalism is the use of plants to treat ailments. Herbal remedies come in a variety of forms – capsules, tinctures, infusions, decoctions, ointments and compresses. Consult a herbalist before taking any specific remedies, particularly if you are pregnant. Contact the General Council and Register of Consultant Herbalists, Grosvenor House, 40 Sea Way, Middleton-on-Sea, West Sussex PO22 7SA or the National Institute of Medical Herbalists, 9 Palace Gate, Exeter EX1 1JA. Here are some herbal remedies obtainable in capsule form from chemists and health-food shops:

- Garlic – often called 'nature's antibiotic', it is marvellous for cleansing the blood and enhances immune responses. It is usually deodorized.
- Ethinacea – very good for colds and flu as it has antiviral and antibacterial properties.
- Eyebright – relieves discomfort of eyestrain or minor eye irritations and hay fever.
- Evening primrose oil – helps nourish skin and relieves symptoms connected with the menopause.
- Korean ginseng – known as 'the queen of herbs', it is probably the oldest and most widely used herb in the world. Slowly builds energy and stamina over a period of weeks.
- Barley tablets – an excellent source of vitamins, proteins and minerals.
- Feverfew – alleviates migraines, headaches and menstrual pain.
- Red raspberry leaves – help strengthen the uterine wall, aiding delivery in childbirth as well as assuaging period pains and curing heavy periods.
- Ginger – used in the east for over 2000 years, it helps stimulate the circulation and relaxes blood vessels.
- Liquorice root – aids digestion, as it limits the production of acid in the system.
- Yucca – helps alleviate the problems of arthritis, rheumatism and gout.
- Kelp – rich in calcium, potassium and magnesium; wonderful for hair and nails.
- Dandelion root – a diuretic and a good tonic for the liver.
- Red clover – good for chronic skin problems such as eczema and psoriasis.
- Royal jelly – a good source of energy.

Herbal teas are a marvellous alternative to drinking lots of coffee or traditional tea as they are caffeine-free and have beneficial properties:

- Camomile – helps you relax and aids digestion. Best drank at bedtime.
- Peppermint – helps inject a bit of 'pep', as the name implies. Also aids digestion.
- Lemon – highly refreshing and contains vitamin C.
- Nettle – helps relieve the symptoms of hay fever.

A wide variety of fruit teas is also available. These are also caffeine-free.

Massage

Massage is a wonderful way in which to relax. If you are frantically busy, try to find time for a regular massage (possibly during your lunch hour), as the amount of energy that can be restored by a period of deep relaxation is enormous. A massage will not only help relax tense muscles and calm frayed nerves, it will also stimulate the blood supply and help release toxins that build up in the muscles. After a massage, drink plenty of water to enable your system to flush out as much waste as possible. As with all therapists, choose a massage practitioner whose certificate of competence is prominently displayed.

Reflexology

Reflexology is a stimulating and revitalizing experience, and can be of real benefit, especially in times of stress. This therapy is based on the theory that energy channels, known as zones or meridians, pass through every organ of the body and end in the feet, which contain 72,000 nerve endings. The Chinese have used this treatment for thousands of years and it is becoming increasingly popular in the west. By massaging specific areas of the feet, reflexologists are able to work on corresponding areas of the body. It can prove beneficial for many complaints, such as backache, premenstrual syndrome, migraine, acne, eczema and psoriasis. I visited a reflexologist when I was suffering from a slight kidney infection. When the reflexologist came to massage that particular point of the foot, it was uncomfortable. She advised me to see my doctor to be on the safe side, but after the massage I felt a lot better.

EXERCISE

Although statistics tell us that, in the west, we eat less now than we did twenty years ago, obesity is an increasing problem. The reason seems to be lack of exercise. An important part of presenting a positive image is being fit and energetic, whatever size we are, and a regular exercise routine is essential if we are to achieve this.

If, like me, the thought of jogging for miles appalls you and you cannot get near a gym, you can still build exercise into your daily routine. Try to cycle instead of using the car, for example, and take the stairs rather than the lift. If you have any damaged muscles or joints, walking and swimming are the best forms of exercise. If you are going to do a lot of walking, ensure you have proper cushioned shoes.

There are also exercises that you can do at home. Even ten minutes of exercise every other day is better than nothing. If you do not have a fitness plan or much time, try the routine outlined below. Put on your favourite music to help you exercise rhythmically. Choose music that has a steady beat, but is not too fast (I like the Rolling Stones, James Brown or any soul music). It is essential that you are comfortable with the speed of each exercise.

These exercises may be short and sweet, but I have devised them with the help of Sheena Storah, a Chartered Physiotherapist, who has a special interest in exercise and rehabilitation. She also kept Lancashire County Cricketers on their feet for over six years! These exercises do work on every part of your body and you can extend them as you wish. If you do nothing else, try and manage the stretching, as it will pay dividends.

1   Always start by gently warming up. March on the spot or step on and off the bottom stair or a shallow step for about four minutes. Next comes the stretch. Try to touch the ceiling! Reach up as high as you can until you feel your spine lengthen, being careful not to push your head back too far, as this can strain the neck. Do this to the count of twenty.

2   Stand with your legs apart, put your hands on your hips and, keeping your back straight, bend your knees, keeping them in line with the toes. Repeat twenty times.

3   Keeping your hands on your hips and your back straight, gently swing the body from side to side, twenty times.

4   Put your hands in the air and stretch up, then drop your arms towards your toes. Lower your head and shoulders towards the floor with knees slightly bent. Try this ten times.

5   Place fingertips together level with your bust and push your arms back twenty times. Next, spread the arms out horizontally and back another twenty times.

6   Stretch your arms out in front of you, cross them at the wrist with palms facing, and then clasp hands together. Raise both arms above your head and stretch up as far as you can. Now 'pulse' them twenty times.

7   Lie flat on the floor and bring each knee up to your chin in turn, twenty times.

8   Stay on the floor with your knees bent. Flatten the hollow of your back into the floor, pulling your tummy in tight. Gently lift your head and shoulders a little, twenty times.

9   Stand up slowly. With both hands, hold on to a sturdy piece of furniture (the dining-room table or a chest of drawers), arms outstretched. Raise one leg behind you, then the other. Repeat twenty times.

10   Run on the spot for as long as you can before it feels uncomfortable.

There are also all kinds of fitness tapes and videos available, so try and find one that works for you. Jane Fonda has produced several, as has Callan Pinkney, the founder of Callanetics.

Keeping fit really is essential as far as prolonging life is concerned. If you are at all worried about starting an exercise regime, go and see your doctor first. If you keep fit you feel well, and if you feel well, you look good!

first impressions

Whether we like it or not, the way we look influences the way in which we are perceived and received by others. Police descriptions of suspects always mention their clothes, size and colouring, as these are the first things we notice. First impressions are powerful. If our first impression of someone is negative, it will stay with us for a long time, making it very difficult to replace it with a positive image. And it is not just our appearance that creates the first impression – analysts claim that our reaction to others is judged thus:

- 58 per cent on how we look.
- 35 per cent on how we sound.
- 7 per cent on what we say.

You have to decide what image you want to impress upon people, and try to make sure you achieve it. This can, however, be difficult. If, for example, you are at the beginning of your career, you might not yet be sure of the image you want to portray. And if you have spent the last seven or eight years bringing up children, your self-image is probably that of a mother, which, let's face it, is a very important job in its own right. You do, however, have to wear two hats when you are a working mum, and the impression at work must be that of a professional woman.

When a job interview is looming, it is important to look the part, but it is also vital not to dress or talk yourself out of a job. Think of the impression you are giving a prospective employer. If you behave as though you are after her job and dress as if you are a member of the board, it might not go down too well. For more on interview technique, *see Chapter 5*.

First impressions can have a significant effect on various aspects of your life, some more serious than others. As far as the law is concerned, the trial of O. J. Simpson provided an interesting example. It was at that time that American lawyers started doing 'make-overs' on witnesses so that they promoted a positive image and were more acceptable to juries. Whether this was right or wrong, it shows the power and importance of the image you project and the impression you leave.

We make immediate judgements about whom we want to talk to based on appearance and body language. This is followed by how people sound, not by what they are saying. Whether someone is small or tall, fat or thin all has a bearing on how we react to that person. A small, delicate, blue-eyed blonde may be really dynamic, but if she speaks in a high, soft voice, people will not take her seriously. You have to be aware of how your basic physique comes across and compensate for it if necessary.

When people say 'Oh, you're not what I expected at all!', ask them why, and find out how they did picture you. It is a good thing to stand back and let other people tell you how they see you, as we all have a set idea of the image we portray to the world, but it might not be the one we think it is.

THE VISUAL IMAGE

The visual image is very important as it is the first image people have of you before you open your mouth. Communication comes from the face and the eyes, and a person's attractiveness is down to their expression, not the way their features are arranged. Thinking positive thoughts will help determine a positive impression, especially as we get older, because our thoughts show on our face. Comedian Ken Dodd says that the shortest distance between two people is a smile! A smiling face is an appealing face, giving an agreeable first impression. A really bright smile can have an amazing effect. It can light up a plain face and, more importantly, break down the invisible barriers that exist between us all.

Our expressions can have a material effect on the way we think and the way we feel. Some psychologists claim that different expressions affect the flow of blood to the brain, causing positive or negative feelings. Laughter and smiling are said to increase the flow, producing positive emotions. It's worth a try anyway!

For a smile to create a positive impression, it must be genuine. There are several types of smile:

- A genuine smile is shown by both corners of the mouth turning up. Sometimes the teeth are shown and sometimes not.
- The miserable smile is hiding distress or unhappiness, usually as a front before others. It is characterized by a lack of symmetry, with one side seeming not to smile at all.
- The false smile signals insincerity. It usually lasts longer than a real one and does not reach the eyes, which remain cold or hard.

A good, strong smile is a winning asset, so do not be afraid to use it! Laughter, too, is strong medicine, helping us to achieve a natural high and a release from tension, which is why some people (especially children) laugh when they are in trouble. It is said that one minute of laughter can provide up to forty-five minutes of relaxation, enabling the body to unwind. Happy people not only appear more relaxed – they usually are.

Your clothes and general appearance will also create a strong first impression. People will instantly decide whether you are a tidy or untidy person, imaginative or chic. If you are pretty, blonde and wear high heels you could be thought of as an airhead. If you wear glasses and your hair is long and straight, or put up in a bun, you might be classified as 'intellectual'. If you have very short hair and wear a tie and trousers, your sexuality could be called into question. They are very obvious stereotypes, but I mention them because these things should go through your mind when you are trying to make a positive first impression. The person you are about to meet does not know you, and may know nothing about you, so his or her initial judgement will be based on how you look.

Men get more of a chance to speak their way into a situation, whereas first impressions of women tend to be formed by their appearance. Black or dark colours are still perceived to be professional. If you are being interviewed for a job in one of the 'professions', you can make an impression without going over the top by choosing plum, olive or another subtle colour. Pastel shades used to be associated with 'bimbos', but this does not apply so much these days. Whatever colour you wear, your colouring and personality will also send out messages. For example, a brunette wearing sugar-pink will transmit a stronger image than a blonde wearing the same colour. If you want to make an impact, wear something bright and colourful. Do not wear dull, grey clothes that blend into the background.

Image Consultants

If you are unsure of the impression you are making, there are firms of image consultants all over the country who will check the colours that suit you and give useful advice. 'Color Me Beautiful' (CMB), 66 Abbey Business Centre, Ingate Place, London SW8 3NS, has a list of consultants available throughout the UK as does 'First Impressions', The Coach House, Ramsey Manor, 37 High Street, Burwell CB5 0HD. Image consultants will take your occupation and lifestyle into consideration, and advise you on how to dress appropriately. Although you want to create a positive impression, it is important that what you wear does not distract others from what you do. If you are giving a presentation, for example, you do not want other women to say 'I didn't like that suit' rather than 'that was a very interesting point she made'. This means dressing to suit the occasion, whatever that may be. If you wore a long, flowing skirt and sandals for a board meeting, you probably would not be taken seriously. When discussing redundancies, a shocking-pink suit and stilettos would most certainly send out the wrong signals. A Tory councillor wearing a hat has to be aware that she immediately shouts middle-class values, and a doctor dressed in jeans and a T-shirt, rather than a crisp white coat, might have difficulty in gaining the trust of her patients.

Ethnic Issues

Sadly, racism does exist, and when you apply for a job it is a potential issue which cannot be ignored. The colour of someone's skin obviously makes an impression. A white person applying for a job cooking in a Chinese restaurant would have more difficulty convincing the owner that she was right for the post than someone from Hong Kong. Whatever the colour of your skin, it is essential to put forward your positive points, be realistic about the role you are pursuing and believe in yourself. If you are right for the position and that firm does not employ you, then they are the ones who are losing out.

Dillis Viney is a consultant in human resources with the London firm, Towers Perrin. Her aim is to become the top black female partner. She told me: 'Black women tend to take the lead in both Afro-Caribbean and African societies, and because of this they are tending to be higher achievers than men at the moment. My mother was very pushy. Her attitude was: because you are black, because you are a girl, you have got to do better than everyone else. My sisters and I didn't go out to discos when we were young; we had to concentrate on our "A" levels. I don't think I had my first real boyfriend until the age of 21!' Her father was also very ambitious for her, which she sees as a vital contribution to her success. If she has come across any racism she has been unaware of it, and she never expects it.

However much you want to wear traditional dress, the stereotyping of black and Asian women may heighten employers' preconceptions of how they expect you to behave. Their first impression might be one of doubt as to whether you will fit in culturally with the organization. That goes for any sort of national dress – if you turned up for an interview wearing a kilt or lederhosen, the effect would be the same. When that crucial first impression is being formed, people tend to warm to those whom they perceive as like-minded. Education, tolerance and understanding regarding different cultures are vital if we are going to progress in the future.

Style

Style of dress makes an immediate impression, and this is especially true for women. It is an unfortunate fact that, as we get older, we are deemed to lose our senses as well as our looks. So if our clothes are out of date, it is assumed that our ideas probably are too! This does not happen to men, and it is as untrue as it is unfair. But it does mean that it is important to move with the times. It is not necessary to wear a miniskirt if you are over fifty, but it might mean throwing out or altering a jacket with shoulder pads that were the height of fashion in the 1980s.

Earlier I touched on what makes 'style', but how do you achieve it? The first thing is to keep your clothes in excellent condition. They must always be clean – a line of make-up round a collar will ruin an otherwise stylish ensemble. Creases, tears, holes, stains, loose buttons, uneven hemlines or laddered tights all help make a negative first impression, and definitely have no style at all! Being stylish takes time and effort. You need to check your clothes regularly to ensure they are in tip-top condition whenever you need them.

When putting together stylish outfits you need to be aware of your body measurements, personality and budget. Take a look in the mirror and measure your height, bust, hips, the length of your torso from under your arms to the waist and the length of your legs. Next, find out what colours suit you. If you are not sure – ask! If you do not want to go to image consultants, ask friends, family, shop assistants and colleagues. When you have decided on your colour range, buy clothes that will mix and match. Take, for example, a pair of trousers. Why not look for a colour and style that will go with a particular:

- jacket
- jersey
- T-shirt
- blouse?

Add different belts and shoes, and you now have four different outfits. Do the same with skirts, shorts, jerseys, jeans, shirts and blouses. You might think that choosing something like a T-shirt is simple; but to give the outfit 'style' there needs to be a theme, whether it is the cut, the pattern or the colour. If you have a checked or patterned shirt, pick out one of the exact colours for the trousers, not something that nearly matches. If you are wearing a highly tailored jacket, the skirt or trousers need to be tailored too. If the dress you are wearing is of a soft, flowing material, then a heavy wool jacket would not complement it.

However good a particular item of clothing may be, if you have nothing to wear it with, it is a waste of money because it will never look right. A beautiful jacket that is either the wrong colour or the wrong style to complement anything in your wardrobe will sit there all year. A pair of shoes that do not quite suit any of your skirts or dresses will never be worn.

But what about the cut that will make the most of your particular build? The only way to find out what flatters you most is to try things on. Bear in mind that your body shape is likely to change with age, so the clothes that suited you ten years ago may be unflattering now. It is a good idea to put on things that you cannot afford as well as those you can. It may be rather frustrating, but it will help you gain a concept of quality and cut, and give you something to save up for!

Dressing smartly when you are shopping for clothes means you will be treated with more respect and therefore get much better service. You should also wear the type of shoes that will go with the outfit you intend to buy, otherwise you will not see the whole picture.

Assistants are there to sell the clothes, but if you tell them that you are trying to establish a particular style, they are usually helpful and should give reasonably unbiased advice. If you cannot find an indefatigable friend to go with you, trust your own judgement; if you think something looks awful then it probably does!

Age and personality have a lot to do with style. However much you may want to wear trendy, up-to-the-minute fashion that will get you noticed, you will never look 'stylish' if you feel uncomfortable. You have to be able to wear your clothes with pride and confidence. The most stunning outfit worn by somebody with drooping shoulders and a hanging head will look nothing, whereas a dress from C&A worn with unusual accessories and confidence can look a million dollars. You can put your own touches to any outfit by adding:

- a distinctive brooch
- an unusual belt or pair of shoes
- a scarf or shawl
- a special necklace or pair of earrings
- beautiful buttons
- an exquisite hat.

Clothes should be worn like a second skin, reflecting your mood and character. If you go out of the door first thing in the morning knowing you are wearing the wrong thing, it can affect your performance all day; so go back in and change! But whether you are going out to paint the town or merely to shop in the supermarket, your clothes must be clean, pressed, co-ordinated and distinctive to create that certain something called 'style'.

Clothes Shopping

While I cannot give individual advice as to where you might shop for your clothes, here are some guidelines. I have not included designer clothes in this section.

18–25 Age Range

You can get away with almost anything when you are young, so shop around and mix some expensive items with cheaper ones. Try:

- River Island
- Oasis
- Jigsaw
- Warehouse
- In Wear
- Miss Selfridge

25–45 Age Range

You are probably spending a little more on specific outfits as you progress up the ladder. Quality rather than quantity should be the order of the day. Try:

- Next
- Monsoon
- Principles
- Marks and Spencer
- Laura Ashley
- French Connection
- Wallis
- Oui Set
- Jaeger

45-plus Age Range

You are probably still shopping at many of the above if you are in your forties or fifties, but here are a few more suggestions:

- Jacques Vert
- Aquascutum
- Eastex
- Bernard Wetherill

Style on a Budget

We all need to know how to make the right impression without breaking the bank, so here are a few tips for a very basic capsule wardrobe for work:

- a well-cut blazer
- two skirts – one black or navy

- a dress that will go with the blazer
- a pair of trousers
- a blouse and a shirt and a couple of bodies to match the skirts and trousers
- two scarves – one small and one large
- a medium-sized handbag
- two different belts
- black court shoes
- a warm coat or mac.

Your working wardrobe obviously depends on what line of employment you are in, but this is the absolute minimum you can get away with to look professional for most jobs, and it will cost you anything from £400. If you can plan ahead, buy in the sales in order to pick up some bargains and really save money.

Body Language

How we behave is as important as what we wear. The way we enter a room, the way we stand and sit and the way we speak all help to create that first impression. Chapter 3 looks at improving body language and vocal technique, but for now we will concentrate on the positive and negative conclusions that can be drawn from how we conduct ourselves.

Nerves

There are several clues that tell us when someone is nervous. A dry mouth, licking of the lips, throat clearing, foot tapping, scratching and rapid breathing are obvious signs, and they can give a very negative impression. I will be giving some tips on controlling nerves in Chapters 5 and 6.

Touch

Our skin is a massive sensory organ sending messages to the brain. Touch is very important to most animals, especially humans. We all feel better when we have had some sun on our backs, and a massage leaves the body feeling both stimulated and relaxed. Tactile people are often more popular than those who never touch, as it enables us, both consciously and subconsciously, to get closer to each other.

We have to be careful not to invade someone's personal space, but a brief squeeze of the hand or a touch on the arm can do much to reassure, comfort or cajole.

Stance

When you walk into a room, stand tall with your head up and your gaze directed at the person to whom you are going to talk. This automatically makes you look and feel confident and at ease. It does not mean putting your nose in the air (which gives the impression of haughtiness), but standing with your shoulders back and your head facing forward. If you have initiated the meeting, walk towards the other person and offer your hand.

The Handshake

A firm handshake is vital. I certainly find it makes a strong impression on me. If someone in a powerful position offers me a 'limp lettuce' or a 'wet fish', I always question how they got where they did, and wonder where their weak point is. Some women today tend to go overboard and are almost fierce in the way they grasp your unsuspecting paw. There is no need to overdo it! It is quite sufficient to take the hand, clasp it firmly and then let go. It can be interesting to watch out for personality traits in the way a hand is proffered:

- The person to offer the hand first is generally the most assertive.
- The strength of contact can be an indicator of character.
- If no hand is offered in return, that person is either very shy, has a hygiene phobia or is trying to put you down!
- A dominant handshake is offered with the palm face down.
- A submissive handshake is when the palm faces up.
- Aim for equal status – arm outstretched with the hand horizontal, thumb facing upwards.

Posture

There is a big difference between confidence and arrogance. Overconfidence or superiority is often displayed by the way someone sits. This could be with the hands clasped behind the head, or leaning back in the chair with legs outstretched and ankles crossed. A prospective employer or future client adopting this position could well be playing for effect to see how you react to such rudeness. Someone who is sitting forward in the chair or leaning on a desk, perhaps forming a 'steeple' with the fingers, is much more likely to be listening with interest to what you have to say. Glasses often have a role to play. Some people gain thinking time by polishing their glasses or slowly and deliberately folding them before asking the next question.

To create a positive impression you should aim to:

- Look alert.
- Sit straight (without looking as though you have a poker down your back).
- Keep your head up, with your eye line directed at the person in front of you.
- Keep hands clasped on your lap unless you are taking notes.
- Cross your legs at the ankles, one knee over the other and legs slightly to one side, or knees and ankles together.

Obviously, the more familiar you are with the people and the circumstances, the more your posture will relax.

Eye Contact

Eye contact is critical. You cannot read another person's character unless you can see into his or her eyes. Our pupils unconsciously dilate when we find somebody attractive, and we look into their eyes for longer. But watch out for shifts in eye contact; it could mean that you are starting to talk too much. Aim for a direct gaze but not an unblinking stare. When we are speaking to someone we automatically look first into one eye, then the other, down to the mouth and back to the eyes again, so you can consciously alter your eye line if you are becoming uncomfortable.

Where to Sit

Where you sit, especially in a sales or interview situation, can make quite an impression. For a friendly meeting or chat, the best position is to sit diagonally across a table. If you want to encourage trust, sit next to someone as it is less confrontational. If you want to negotiate a deal, it is best not to sit opposite your potential customer as this can encourage competitive feelings; again, a diagonal position is best.

Reading Body Language

I am sure you have been to parties where you knew instantly that you were not going to enjoy the evening. And you have probably been to interviews where, the minute you walked into the reception, you knew you would not fit in to that company.

The impression a person, a place or an organization makes on you is very important. Try to beware of jumping to instant conclusions, however, especially about people. Some of us are better at evaluating our fellows than others, and although we should take notice of initial reactions, they must not prejudice us against exploring further. This is particularly the case if you are taking part in the selection process for jobs. A candidate for a teaching post, for example, may not initially give the impression that he or she could control a class of unruly adolescents. Further investigation, however, may confirm that the candidate has proved more than a match for the situation in the past and is exactly right for the job.

How do you spot someone who is insincere or lying? Simple things like a shifty gaze and fidgety gestures should put you on your guard. So should a lot of face touching or pulling of the ear lobes. This habit usually stems from childhood – children will cover their mouths when lying, almost as if they want to stop the words coming out. Reading body language has to be done with great caution, however, and the particular circumstances taken into account. An untruthful person often crosses both the arms and legs simultaneously when telling a lie, but so does someone who is in a hurry and wants the conversation to close, or very tired and is trying to inject some adrenaline into their system.

When we talk, most of us use our hands to emphasize points, and the way in which we use them can be very revealing. When someone is lying they tend to clasp the hands together or push them deep into their pockets in case their hands give them away. An indication that the hands are disagreeing with the mouth is evident when the palms face upwards in what is known as the 'hand-shrug'. If somebody is unsure of their facts they will often use this gesture.

Positive Gestures

You cannot manufacture positive body language. If you try to do so, it will have the opposite effect, giving an impression of insincerity. If you are sincere and truthful, it will show. There are, however, positive signs to look out for in others:

- Hand resting on the cheek – means evaluation or analysis.
- Hand stroking chin – signals consideration.
- Steepling the fingers – displays confidence.
- Rubbing hands together quickly – anticipation!
- Hands pressed together – persuasion.

- Leaning forward – denotes active listening.
- Direct eye contact – indicates honesty and interest.
- Eyebrow lift – this quick movement says someone is glad to see you.
- Head held up – marks confidence and integrity.
- A smile – the genuine article shows a sincere greeting.

Personal chemistry matters enormously in your dealings with people – on a professional and a social level – so try to listen to what other people have to say and put yourself in their position before you make up too much of your mind about them. Consider the whole case; do not just go on the first impression.

Gestures to Avoid

Body language must be sincere in order to create the right impression. It is vital that the mind and body are in agreement when we speak, as anyone who has read even a little on the subject will see something that will give us away! Avoid the following negative gestures:

- Fidgeting with the hands.
- Rubbing the nose or eyes.
- Rubbing the hands slowly together (this often denotes lying or insincerity).
- Excessive stroking of the cheek or chin.
- Crossing arms over the chest (forming the 'barrier' position).
- Clenched fists.
- Shifty eye contact.
- Foot tapping.
- Moving the ankles from side to side.
- Too much crossing of arms and legs.

Sexual Signals

Much of our positive body language happens unconsciously, and the way we react to people shows itself in different ways. A man will often begin to smarten himself up at the approach of an attractive woman – a bit like a male bird fluffing out its feathers. Adjusting clothes, straightening the tie and smoothing the hair are all signs of interest, and help make what he hopes will be a positive first impression.

Signs of overt sexual interest are indicated by thumbs thrust into a belt with the hands pointing to the spot marked X, or a hand in the pocket, which is more subtly pointing the same way. If you look at advertisements for men's clothes, the model very often stands with one hand in his jacket or trouser pocket. Feet, too, can show the direction a man's thoughts are taking. If he is interested or curious about you, one or both feet will be pointed in your direction, even if the rest of his body is not. This also applies to single-sex groups, where it will show empathy or interest.

Women, as well as men, rearrange their clothes and tidy their hair if they are approached by somebody they find attractive; and our feet, too, act as indicators of interest or sympathy. We also tend to push up our sleeves, thus revealing the soft, vulnerable skin on the inside of our wrists while using hand movements that point towards the person in whom we are interested. When sitting, we tend to cross and uncross our legs more slowly, especially if we are wearing a short skirt, as it shows the legs off to their best advantage.

Stroking thighs and pushing a foot in and out of a shoe display quite strong signs of sexual attraction, and we are often oblivious to the fact that we are doing anything at all. Both sexes will play with objects when getting to know one another. It can be fascinating to watch couples having dinner, for instance. Either sex can find themselves doing something extremely Freudian with the stem of a wine glass or an unsuspecting saltcellar! Watch, too, how the glass will be subconsciously pushed backwards and forwards as the course of the conversation changes, and the allure ebbs and flows.

In these days of sexual equality, with women wearing the trousers (both figuratively and literally), we are adopting a more aggressive stance, showing overt signs of interest in the opposite sex. Women frequently stand and sit with their legs apart, but there is still a taboo attached to exaggerated examples of this sort of stance, as it signals a rather crude 'come and get me' attitude which is unattractive to both sexes. An aggressive posture, such as a woman standing with legs apart and hands on hips is often used in advertisements to create a sexy image. Many women reading this might scoff at the idea that we are so transparent in our sexual behaviour – but look around the next time you are at a party or attending a meeting. You will be surprised just how easy it is to tell who fancies whom! It is as well to bear in mind that, depending on the age group, most men feel threatened by blatant sexual behaviour in women, as it makes them less confident.

THE VOCAL IMAGE

I expect we have all formed a vocal image of someone at some time or another. It might be a client at the end of the telephone or an actor on the radio. Very often the voice and the physique do not match up, which can sometimes be quite disappointing!

Chapter 3 looks in more detail at the voice and what we can do to improve both range and expression. The voice is our most powerful instrument of communication, and it is vital that we use it well. A woman with a high-pitched, grating voice or a very strong regional accent will have to work harder to create a positive impression than a woman whose voice is warm, modulated and easily understood.

It is important not to speak too quickly. Nerves often cause us to speed up, which can be off-putting for others. It is a good thought to rehearse what you are going to say when you first meet someone, even if it is only 'hello' and stating your name.

You never get a second chance to make a first impression, so remember to:

- Choose clothes suitable for the occasion.
- Stand tall when you enter a room.
- Look the other person in the eye.
- Give a firm handshake.
- Know what you are going to say.

3

building confidence

Confidence is something we all lack at some time in our lives. Even the most assured-looking women are probably quaking in their shoes at the thought of giving a major presentation or facing an important interview. People often say to me 'you never seem to be nervous', despite the fact that I suffer from nerves as much as the next woman. I always think of a phrase one of my partners in Public Image uses when advising people on coping with nerves: 'people would worry less about what others thought about them if they realized how seldom they do'. We are all self-centred beings who focus most of our attention on ourselves most of the time.

Having said that, self-confidence is vital if we are to succeed in our domestic and work life. A presentation that fails miserably because your voice faltered and your eye line never left your notes can leave a lasting negative impression on both you and your audience. A boss who constantly checks everything you do undermines your confidence. A woman who is constantly put down by her husband lacks self-esteem. It is important to analyse why we feel the way we do, as there are different ways of boosting morale.

There are three steps to becoming confident.

1   Facing our fears.
2   Gaining self-knowledge.
3   Positive thinking.

If people lack confidence, they have a fear for a specific reason. It may be that they fear they will be laughed at. They may worry they will look ridiculous, or be apprehensive that they are not as good as someone else at a specific task. Whatever your anxieties, facing up to them is vital. Ask yourself:

Have I always lacked confidence?
When did I begin to lose it?

Then examine the reasons why it is lacking and look for ways of regaining it. You can do this in different ways:

visualization
discarding negative thoughts
improving weaknesses
relaxation.

Be positive! Try envisaging the best out of a situation. If you think you are going to fail, you are much more likely to do so. If you anticipate a disaster, there will probably be one. Strive to make yourself look forward to the circumstances, whatever they are, and visualize success beforehand. This technique can be used in every situation, even a confrontation with the children. If you expect to have a problem getting them off to school, then you will. It might be naively optimistic in some situations, but a positive focus to your life is contagious.

Getting to know and acknowledge your weak points is also important. You may hate public speaking, but if it is part of your job, make sure you get help. Many companies offer presentation training. Track them down via your local telephone directory or, better still, ask around, as personal recommendation is the best guide. Public Image mounts open courses once a month, as well as those run in-house for specific organizations. Badger your boss into sending you on a course. If you are self-employed, seek expert advice.

Situations you are unsure about are sometimes better avoided. If something is very stressful and you know you are not going to be able to cope, look at alternatives. Face-to-face confrontation might be anathema to you, for example; in that case write a letter or a memo, so that you can say what you mean without feeling you are going to lose control of the situation.

Give yourself the time and the environment to think clearly and put your point across. If you find that negotiating is a weak point, write down the outcome that you are looking for and stick to it. If it is a price, for instance, and you are worried that you are going to be beaten down, you might say something like this to your customer: 'Well, Mr Brown. Having researched the situation fully, I feel this is the right price for all concerned. To come down any further would mean a diminution of both quality and service, which would be to no one's advantage. We will guarantee to deliver your order on time every month, and I know you will be delighted with the quality...'. Have the confidence to follow your own judgement. Both positivity and negativity are communicable and pass from person to person. Try to absorb the positive and disregard the negative.

We all have something that perks us up a bit when we are down. If you are feeling particularly apprehensive, give yourself a treat. It might be a forbidden chocolate bar, a splash of your favourite perfume, having your hair done or using a bright lipstick. I always feel good if I have nice nails. A new piece of lingerie or jewellery is also a tonic. Tara Newley, singer and radio presenter, dresses to impress every day: 'If I don't think I look good, I don't feel good. If I feel I have made an effort with my appearance, it gives me confidence.'

Dillis Viney, Management Consultant with Towers Perrin in London, has been lucky in that her parents have been supportive, giving her a strong self-image and telling her she was capable of achieving what she wanted to achieve. 'Before I went off for an interview, if I had any doubts, my mother would say how wonderful I was, which gave me enormous confidence.' Endeavour to be as supportive as possible to your partner, your children and – it may sound odd – to yourself. We are very good at knocking ourselves and wondering whether we have the right to expect success; but we have every right and should seek to achieve it.

Focus on your good points. You can help build confidence by making a list of your:

strengths
talents
skills
achievements.

These could be in any field, either domestic or in the workplace. I cannot stress heavily enough that everybody has abilities and accomplishments of which they can be proud. Think about yours and focus on them.

PRESENTING A CONFIDENT IMAGE

Dressing with Confidence

If you know you are wearing the 'right' clothes and look good, you will feel confident on any occasion, whether social or professional. But what is 'right'? An outfit suitable for a day at Ascot races might not be fitting for a day watching tennis at Wimbledon. Corporate entertaining still plays an important part in making contacts and getting business, so whether you are there as part of your organization or as a guest with a partner, it is essential that you look right if you are going to feel confident. Although etiquette and dress codes are not as rigid as they once were, there are still certain guidelines that should be followed to create the appropriate image. Chapter 8 looks at this subject in more detail.

Speaking with Confidence

Your voice plays a huge part in projecting confidence. A tell-tale tremor can sow seeds of doubt as to the validity of what you are saying, whilst a monotonous drone will turn anybody off. Good diction is important, otherwise people will have difficulty in hearing what you are saying, leading to unnecessary misunderstandings and poor communication. Accents, as I have said, can cause bias, especially if they are very strong; but they should not be a problem unless they are difficult for anyone outside that region to comprehend. Unless you feel that you are at a disadvantage from betraying your origins, I would not attempt to lose an accent. If, however, you feel uncertain because of it, there are exercises and tuition available to help you speak 'standard English'.

Here are some procedures to improve diction, and help train the mind and mouth to work together at the same speed. I hope these tips will be of assistance in everyday conversation at work or at home, not just when preparing for an interview or a presentation, as good communication is vital to success in any field.

It is important to remember that the sound we hear in our own head is not necessarily the one other people hear, so if possible, read these exercises into a reasonably good tape recorder (not a Dictaphone) so that you can get to know your voice and monitor the improvement.

All these exercises work on different levels. They rehearse the voice and help you to be more relaxed and confident as well as limbering up all the muscles we use for articulation. They will enable you to achieve strong, clear speech if practised regularly.

Expression

If a voice has no expression, no one will listen to it, no matter how important the message. It is therefore vital that we learn to use the vocal range that we all possess to its full advantage.

> Say aloud: 'That was a nice meal.'
> With more feeling: 'That was a lovely meal.'
> Aim the pitch at the top: 'That was a delicious meal.'
> Normal: 'That was a nice meal.'
> Down in pitch: 'That was an average meal.'
> Right down: 'That was a disgusting meal.'

Another useful exercise is to read a section of the newspaper into a tape recorder in several different ways. As if:

> You are speaking at a wedding.
> You are speaking at a funeral.
> You are addressing a large crowd.
> You are talking to a group of children.

The same text should sound completely different each time you read it, proving that it is not just what you say that is important, but the way you say it. Try reading this sentence, stressing each word in capitals.

> DID you invite him for lunch?
> Did YOU invite him for lunch?
> Did you INVITE him for lunch?
> Did you invite HIM for lunch?
> Did you invite him FOR lunch?
> Did you invite him for LUNCH?

The emphasis dictates the subtle changes in meaning of the sentence, so analyse the text and stress the relevant words.

If you have young children, tape record the stories you read to them, especially the ones where there are a number of characters, so that you can experiment using the whole of your vocal range.

Breath Control

Breathing correctly is essential for good voice control and production. It is important to practise breathing exercises to develop control over the muscles in order to produce your voice at varying volumes, with longer phrasing and ease of speech. When you breathe correctly for speech, the following sequence of events takes place:

1   You breathe in deeply.
2   The diaphragm (a dome-shaped muscle in your chest) descends, the chest moves outwards and upwards and more air fills the lungs.
3   The diaphragm rises again while the ribs stay in the same position and air is expelled.
4   The ribs descend and further air is expelled.
5   Sound is caused by breath striking the vocal cords. It is important to try and be as relaxed as possible. Tensing causes the breath to be shorter and the voice poor.

These exercises will help you control and use your breath properly.

1   Breathe in and say the months of the year as you expel the breath.
2   Try humming and filling the resonators in the head so that you can feel the head throbbing.
3   Read a poem or a passage of prose and mark the places where you need to breathe. Whisper the piece, then gradually increase the volume. Be aware of the lips, mouth and tongue. Practise saying words in an exaggerated way so that you can feel the tongue, lips and mouth moving.
4   Now try using these two phrases (take a deep breath before each sentence):

I can make my voice rise higher and higher and higher.
I can make my voice go deeper and deeper and deeper.

This is another exercise to help you control your breathing. Take a breath after every line:

I
I must
I must control my
I must control my breath
I must control my breath and
I must control my breath and sustain
I must control my breath and sustain my
I must control my breath and sustain my sentences

Clear Speech

Repeat each of the following phrases about three times, beginning with a whisper and increasing the volume through the second and third repeats. Do these exercises occasionally in order to increase the agility of the tongue, lips and mouth. Try to keep the words clear and sharp:

Twist the twine tightly round the tree trunks.
Did Dora dare to deceive David deliberately?
Kate Cooney carefully closed the kitchen cupboards.
Gregory Gartside gained good gradings in Greek grammar.
Naughty Nora has no nice neighbours.
Little Larry Lester lolled lazily on the lilo.
Peggy Babcock.
Red leather, yellow leather, red lorry, yellow lorry.
Unique New York, New York unique.
Fresh fried fish.
A cracked cricket critic.
Try tying the twine round the three tree twigs.
The seething sea ceaseth and thus sufficeth us.
She sells sea shells on the sea shore.
Theophilus Thistle, the successful thistle sifter, in sifting a sieve full of unsifted thistles, thrust three thousand thistles through the thick of his thumb.
How much wood could a woodchuck chuck / If a woodchuck could chuck wood? / As much good wood as a woodchuck could chuck, / If a woodchuck could chuck wood.

Confident Body Language

Stance is vital to portraying confidence. The Pamela Holt Model Agency in Manchester has been helping women and girls gain polish and confidence for the last twenty-five years. In a week they can transform an ugly duckling into a swan with advice on clothes, deportment and make-up. I must say that taking a modelling course is wonderful training, whether you use it professionally or not, and agencies throughout the country run five-day sessions at night as well as during the day. The way you walk and carry yourself is fundamental to displaying clothes to their best advantage and projecting a confident, positive image. Here are a few tips:

Stand tall with your head up. The fact that you are looking people in the eye will help you feel on a par with them.

Roll your shoulders up towards your ears and then down until they rest naturally.

Pull your stomach in.

Tighten your buttocks.

Let your arms hang by your sides, keeping them behind the side-seams of your clothes. This keeps your shoulders back.

Walk with your head up, keeping the weight back, and take steps that feel comfortable – not too long and not too short.

STRESS AND RELAXATION

We all suffer from stress, but it affects different people in different ways. At worst it means days off work or even spells in hospital; at best it makes us feel tired and irritable. But stress has always been part of the human condition. Pain, fear, effort, worry and lack of time are among the many causes. It is impossible to avoid stress, but it is possible to control it using good relaxation techniques.

Relaxation means being at ease, letting go of the tension that often accompanies a busy life. Proper relaxation of both body and mind is essential for health, both in your business and social life. The result is a relaxed, healthy body and a clear mind.

To combat stress try and make more time:

for journeys
to accomplish tasks
for yourself.

Each day, sit quietly or lie down if possible, even if only for a few minutes, and let yourself unwind. Concentrate on your body, on every muscle, as you feel it begin to relax.

The more you are able to relax, the more you will feel able to cope with everyday problems, and this will help increase your confidence and mental energy. There are many courses and workshops run to help people cope with stress, as well as books and tapes on the subject (*see Bibliography*), so you will probably find something that suits you.

Relaxation Exercises

Here are some very simple exercises to relieve some of the aches, pains and overstretched nerves caused by the build-up of stress. These basic exercises can help get rid of tension caused by the everyday niggles of home or work, which combined with rushed appointments, hurried deadlines, missed meals and disobedient children can all add up to stress!

1   Stand or sit comfortably and let your head roll round gently three or four times.
2   Shake your wrists.
3   Breathe in slowly and gradually exhale. Repeat three times.
4   Tense your whole body, clenching your fists and screwing up your face until you can feel yourself trembling – then relax and breathe deeply in and out to the count of three.
5   Raise your arms above your head and stretch to the ceiling, then drop down from the waist, swinging your arms down and bending the knees. Gradually come up again to a standing position. Repeat six times.
6   Roll your shoulders in a circular movement.
7   Raise your shoulders to try to touch the ears. Hold this position, note the tension and release. Do this five times.
8   Push or imagine yourself pushing against a wall about a foot away at shoulder height. Gradually release the effort and allow your arms to fall to your side.

9 Stand in as relaxed a position as possible, making sure your head is comfortable. Place your hands on your lower ribs. Breathe in through the nose to a count of three, but do not tense and raise shoulders. Feel the ribs swing outwards. Hold for three, then exhale for three. Gradually build up the count.

BUILDING CONFIDENCE IN OTHERS

It is important to help build confidence in colleagues, subordinates, partners and children. Giving people a sense of their own worth enables them to develop their personality, achieve their true potential and work to capacity. To encourage this, strive to:

Compliment whenever practicable, on appearance as well as results.
Motivate by encouraging new ideas.
Criticize constructively, pointing out where things have gone wrong and giving guidance on how to improve them.
Praise as much as possible.

As I said to begin with, we all lack confidence at some time, but if you make the most of your good points and recognize the weak ones, you can do much to boost morale. Whatever you are going to do, take time to prepare. This could be for a board meeting or a social gathering. Grant yourself as much time as possible to find out about the personnel, data and environment. As we say in Public Image: whatever the circumstances, preparation is the key to confidence, and confidence is the key to success.

---

what do they want?

This chapter features different organizations and reveals what they are looking for when they are recruiting. Although there is not room in this book to cover every possible career, I have put together what I hope will be useful advice on some of the mainstream career areas, and much of the information is transferable to other sectors. Some of the people to whom I talked are personnel officers or training and development managers; others are those who work in industry or the professions and can give first-hand information as to what qualities are needed for the job, as well as the image required.

For most positions these days, companies have an idea of the image they want for the ideal employee. If that image does not apply to you, then it is fair to say that you are unlikely to be happy working in that organization. How you dress is important, not only for an interview but also when you start the job. You should not try to be what you are not, and if wearing a suit every day is something that will make you feel desperately stifled and uncomfortable, then you should look seriously at an alternative career.

You may think that by dressing in an unconventional way you are showing that you are an individual with an unusual brain, but the message received might be of somebody who is a loner, a potentially difficult person who will not fit in. Inadvertently, you could be giving off all the wrong signals to a potential employer or, if you are looking for promotion, your boss. It is wise to find out as much as possible, as early as possible, about the corporate image. This will tell you not only how you must dress, but also the way in which you are expected to behave and the type of people you will be working with.

There are certain qualities needed for almost any job which employers look for beyond qualifications and a track record. These qualities are relatively easy to identify and there is usually evidence available if candidates have had previous jobs. They are:

- **Resourcefulness:** helps people find ways around problems and seek out solutions. If an employer gives you a project, he or she does not want you to come back every five minutes asking what to do.
- **Resilience:** sees people through in the long term. It is a combination of stamina, being able to cope with the politics of an organization, the capability to overcome barriers and to solve problems time and time again without giving in. Employers need people who are good at coping with change. For management positions, the ability to introduce change is often an asset.
- **Responsibility:** is self-evident from a few well-chosen questions. What do you do in your spare time? What is your position in the family? Have you had to care for siblings while your parents were working? How much did you contribute to the running of the home? All these experiences help mould your character.
- **Vision:** to be successful you need to have vision. Change in management and environment is the norm today, so an indispensable element is the ability to see learning and development as part of your own responsibility. To be curious is part of survival. Never take things for granted and never be afraid to ask the question 'why?'.

Dale Carnegie once said, 'About 15% of one's financial success is due to one's technical knowledge and about 85% is due to skill in human engineering – to personality and the ability to lead people.' John Paul Mitchell Systems Ltd., the hair-care people, have a set of ten points they look for when recruiting. These are an employee's:

1   beliefs
2   values
3   desires
4   drive
5   knowledge
6   eagerness to learn
7   ability to organize and communicate
8   willingness to do more than is asked
9   vividness of imagination
10   approach to exercising powers of choice.

To John Paul Mitchell Systems and many other companies, the right image means having 'elegance, poise and taste'.

THE 'PROFESSIONS'

A career in one of the professions – such as accountancy, chartered surveying, insurance, the law or banking – requires particular qualifications and certain qualities. These professions have undergone many changes over the last decade, and competition for jobs is ever increasing. The number of graduates applying for jobs outnumbers the vacancies. Arthur Andersen, the international accountancy firm, can take the cream of the crop as far as recruitment is concerned. It receives about 400 applications for every job. Nevertheless, many organizations say that they have difficulty finding the 'right' people.

So what will make you the right person? Obviously, certain qualifications are necessary. 'A' levels are important as they are the gateway to university. There is a view, however, that they are the worst predictor of managerial success, or even of a good degree. But they are a discriminator, and various companies put a lot of emphasis on them, even when recruiting undergraduates, because they are the most recent difficult qualification they can assess. Some accountancy and financial services firms, for instance, tend to look at UCAS points and 'A' levels when recruiting graduates.

Accountancy and Financial Services

To train as an accountant you need a good degree – a first or an upper second. Although it can be in any discipline, employers look for maths 'A' level or give a numeracy test at the interview. They also need people with good communication skills who can handle queries diplomatically and mix with clients. The image of female accountants is less dull than their male counterparts, and these days people are encouraged to be individual while still projecting the professional image of their firm.

Chartered Surveying

To fill the post of chartered surveyor you would need a degree in estate management or a qualification from the Royal Institute of Chartered Surveyors, which can be gained by correspondence courses or day-release schemes. Surveying is still a predominantly male environment, but the number of women entering the profession is increasing rapidly, especially women 'returners' – women returning to work after a period spent raising a family.

You do not have to be qualified to be a residential negotiator for an estate agent. This is a good source of part-time work for many women with families. A sound knowledge of the locality, plus flair and personality, good communication skills, enthusiasm and motivation are what is needed to sell houses. The smaller firms are generally looking for someone who will be with them for some time, so loyalty is important. If an employer sees a CV from someone over thirty who has moved jobs a lot, questions as to loyalty and competency immediately spring to mind. If you have changed jobs frequently, make sure you have a plausible explanation. For more on this, *see Chapter 5*.

Insurance

The insurance industry has seen changing fortunes in the last decade. In many organizations, the number of recruits has fallen from hundreds to around twenty per year. In the last couple of years, Royal Insurance has recruited between ten and fifteen graduates for the general insurance training programme out of 600 to 800 applicants. Life is tough!

A great deal of time and effort is put into developing and training managers, so employers are looking for people with vision. A belief that things can be done better and the wish to influence is what they require in a management team, as well as self-belief and belief in the company.

The Legal Profession

Although fifty per cent of trainee solicitors are women, only a small percentage make it to partner level. For family law or will-making, many clients actively seek a woman solicitor, but even today, large commercial clients would probably rather be represented by a male barrister in his late thirties or early forties than by a woman. In court, the image of the female lawyer is still not as strong as that of her male counterpart, so it is critical that she should be seen to have mastered the brief and appear to be in control. If an advocate looks a mess and her case is badly organized, it will annoy the judge and undercut her potential for success.

To become a solicitor you need a degree. Then there are specialist exams: the CPE (Common Professional Exams) if you have not taken a law degree, and the LPC (Legal Practice Course) required by all graduates. This takes another year at a college of law and is followed by two years as a trainee solicitor. Strong debating skills, enthusiasm, adept use of language and a good voice are useful attributes for the legal profession.

Investment Banking

If you have previously worked in investment banking, employers will want to know about the deals you have conducted, and then about your character. They are likely to ask you about your hobbies and outside interests to see whether you would fit in to their culture.

For most banks in the City, high grades for 'A' levels are required, as well as a good spread of GCSEs. It helps to have attended a top university, such as Oxford, Cambridge, Bristol or Edinburgh, as the university you study at is considered as important as the subjects you study. This is not the case with the high-street banks.

To work in the City you have to be prepared for long and irregular hours. Most people start between 7 and 8 a.m. and will not go home until at least 7.30 p.m. Getting home at 3 a.m. and working weekends is not unusual, so you will have to be prepared for your social life to suffer, which can mean a fairly lonely life outside work.

Banks such as NWS PLC employ telesales staff to sell their services. This is a difficult and lonely job requiring staying power (working days of between twelve and fourteen hours are the norm) and the capacity to enjoy telesales. You also need a good voice and the ability to project yourself well.

Qualities
- leadership ability
- motivation
- determination
- enthusiasm
- ability to work well in a team
- loyalty
- ambition
- integrity
- ability to work hard
- conscientiousness
- initiative
- drive
- ability to learn a language

Dress

Dress is usually fairly conservative for the professions, although there are exceptions. Your clothes do not have to be expensive, but they are usually expected to be classic, discreet, elegant and smart. Bright colours are fine as long as you are happy with the fact that they make you stand out.

These dress tips apply to any of the careers highlighted above, or indeed to any office-based job:

- Buy clothes that you can mix and match.
- Choose material that will wear well and does not crease too much.
- Buy clothes that are as expensive as you can comfortably afford.
- Choose sober colours and add a brooch or scarf to brighten things up.
- Remember that most of the professions prefer women to dress like women – feminine yet credible.
- Try to dress to suit everybody and offend nobody.
- Find an outfit that can be worn both at the office and for an evening out, such as a dress and jacket with a colourful scarf.
- Make sure shoes, briefcases and handbags are kept in good condition.
- Remember you are the image of your organization – make it professional!

INDUSTRY

The term 'industry' encompasses such a wide variety of careers that it is possible only to provide general guidelines in this book.

The Chemical Industry

To learn more about women in industry I spoke to one outstanding individual – chemist Helen Sharman, the only British woman to have travelled in space. She was chosen to go on the Russian Soyuz TM–12 space mission in 1991, having fulfilled several criteria: she had to have a flair for languages (as during the training and on board she had to speak Russian), be a certain height, have a high standard of fitness and be a scientist. When I think of astronauts or cosmonauts I envisage military men, and fairly big men at that! Helen is small, slim and full of energy and enthusiasm for her work.

She says that the image people have of scientists, as grey people who work behind closed doors or in labs, is often incorrect. These days, a science degree will regularly open far more doors than an arts degree. A scientific training creates a logical pattern of thought for prospective managers and enables them to look at things objectively, especially when it comes to problem solving. As far as the chemical industry is concerned, Helen thinks it needs brightening up, showing the flair and imagination that is needed by those who work in it. It has had a lot of bad press over the last few years, and that is something it is trying hard to redress.

I asked Helen what it was like to be in space. She said that, apart from having to get used to weightlessness and working in a confined area, what struck her most was the size of the Earth as they orbited every ninety minutes. It took about five minutes to pass from Belfast to Hamburg, about twenty minutes to cross Africa, and forty minutes to go over the Pacific ocean. Her image of the Earth changed quite a lot, as in one way she was surprised how small it was, and in another, how large.

Telecommunications

BT are meticulous in their recruitment process. They do the 'milk round' at universities and are constantly thinking of new ways to attract graduates. For technical jobs, graduates must have at least an upper-second degree. For a non-technical area, the class of degree is not necessarily as important, and qualities such as innovation, determination and communication skills are also taken into consideration.

When filling in an application form for BT, undergraduates are asked to state the class of degree they are expecting. Most people say they are expecting an upper second, although only relatively few students obtain one. It is better to be realistic, even if you are anticipating a lower second. If you say you are expecting a first, then you had better be confident, as it would be seen as an outrageous lie if you did not get one! 'O' levels can sometimes be used as a useful predictor of degree results. In the days before GCSEs, ten high-grade 'O' levels meant you were likely to make a good manager; in all likelihood, 'A' levels will predict the same. A broad spread of GCSEs that includes English and maths is essential if you want to work for BT, as well as three good 'A' levels.

Qualities
- leadership ability
- commercial and business awareness
- motivation
- determination
- communication skills
- ability to work as part of a team
- attention to detail

Dress
In industry, how you dress is more important if your role involves customer liaison. If you are in a technical job where you do not really meet the public, dress is not so significant.

THE MEDIA

Acting
The image of this part of the media is one of glamour, high earnings and 'luvvies'! Although it does have its glamorous side (a small percentage of actors do earn huge amounts of money) and its share of loveable eccentrics, the reality is a tough, overcrowded and precarious occupation. That said, it can also be the most exciting profession in the world. If acting is what you really want to do, it is essential to be realistic about both your ability and your

dedication. If you are going to succeed in the theatre, for example, it is as well to be able to sing, dance and play at least one instrument as well as act!

Acting on television and in films is rather different from theatre work. Television and film actors have to keep themselves alert during time spent hanging around the set while the crew is setting shots and overcoming technical problems. Once the curtain rises in the theatre, you are on! On stage, you are more or less on your own, but in films and on television, many people play a role in creating the final product. Technicians, the camera crew and other behind-the-scenes staff can all contribute towards you and your performance.

There is no better training for an actor than a repertory theatre company. This gives you the invaluable experience of playing different characters throughout the season. You can also study at a good drama school or take a degree at university. One of the advantages of drama school is that agents and directors go to see the end of year productions to find young talent. If you go to university, do a combined degree so that, if things do not go according to plan, you will be qualified to get another job!

Luck plays a great part in success, as does being in the right place at the right time. With so many actors and actresses to choose from, it is often a case of the face fitting the part. A good agent who keeps his or her ear to the ground as well as negotiating the right deal is also crucial.

When actress Jennifer Saunders holds auditions she generally makes up her mind pretty quickly. It helps if somebody projects the right image and looks the part. 'Some casting directors don't bother to find out what the role is and give the actors no help at all. If they look right it is a great help, as our rehearsal schedule is so fast that we have no time to work on creating the character. I need an actor who is as near that character as possible.'

First impressions are considerable, says Jennifer. 'I immediately notice what people are wearing. I expect them to be presentable. If they can't make an effort for the audition, will they make an effort when they work?' Eye contact is vital. Jennifer herself used to be very shy and found it difficult to look people in the eye, 'Which is probably why I didn't get that much work at one time! But certain things put me off immediately. I won't employ anybody with nose or eyebrow rings on principle.' Never mind the image they are projecting, they make her feel sick!

I asked Jennifer whether her own image had changed with success. 'I think people are more intimidated by me now, and I am unbearably cocky when I go into the BBC!' Age as well as success has brought her confidence. She is certainly in a position to call the shots, but she is entirely sympathetic if people look nervous at auditions, and tries to put them at their ease. She is interested in how they project themselves, and how they react to her.

Be careful which parts you accept. If you say yes to everything, you take the good with the bad. To be selective is a luxury, but it is the right thing in the long term if you want to build up a particular image. Get hold of the script before the audition if you can and work on it. Find out about the director, and discover what he or she likes.

As an actor, you set yourself up for criticism, and some people will try to undermine you. It is difficult not to be upset by gossip and bad publicity, but if you really want to become 'famous' you have to ask yourself whether you will be able to stand the pressure of being public property. You have to learn to expect the worst and yet deal with success. This is something that is unfortunately not taught at drama school.

Television and Film

At least 800 graduates apply for every researcher's job at the BBC, and a staggering 59 per cent of all students want to work for the BBC! This is typical of the sort of competition throughout television. For most production jobs, a degree is now required, although the discipline does not matter.

If you are thinking of becoming a radio or television producer, director or presenter, word-processing and computer skills are extremely useful because many people start off in clerical jobs. Work experience, such as in hospital radio or amateur dramatics, is also helpful. Media courses are not essential as most companies retrain new staff anyway, but they can give you useful programme-making experience.

The film business is also fiercely competitive when it comes to applying for jobs. It differs from television, however, in that new companies tend to be formed for each production, which can take well over a year to complete, so everyone is effectively freelance. The television industry is now heading much the same way, with fewer permanent posts and more and more people being employed on fixed-term contracts. Throughout the television and film industry, the ability to work as part of a team is essential, so a friendly nature is important, especially for anyone working in a small organization. Enthusiasm is another key requirement. People must be keen, unafraid of a challenge and prepared to tackle the unusual.

'We are viewed as rather glitzy and slightly avant-garde as an industry,' says Geoff Hackett, former Senior Producer for The Executive Business Channel. 'In fact, much of the work is office based, using the latest technology.' Geoff always wears a suit and reckons that it matters to look smart. 'You are representing the company whenever you are out on location, filming in someone's office or interviewing people in the street.'

For the technical posts in film and television, 'A' levels in maths and English are necessary. If you are applying for the job of a camera operator, for example, and you have not worked in this field before, you need to bring to the interview some proof of your enthusiasm and ability, such as a video you have made or a portfolio of photographs. Knowledge of relevant equipment is vital. If you already have some experience in the industry, and it is a good idea to put together a short show reel of programmes you have worked on.

If you work for a small organization, the image you present to clients is very important. You might be the only person 'on view' to the customer or viewer. If you present a good public image, you will then be remembered and may be invited back again to film. Even the best camera operator or sound recordist in the world will not be employed by some companies if she looks a real mess.

Tara Newley has the advantages and disadvantages of being the daughter of actress Joan Collins and actor and singer Anthony Newley. Going into the music business using her own name was not easy, as people were slightly hostile and tended not to take her seriously. Her name certainly did not open any doors. When her mother became really famous, Tara was about seventeen and had already left home to study in France. She was too proud to accept any help from her parents and started off making the tea for a company that produced pop videos. As their first female 'runner', she was paid £50 a day, and often worked from eight in the morning until past midnight. It was wonderful experience, and a good way to learn about the film industry. She went on to become a tape operator in a recording studio and PA to the director on the mini-series 'Lace 2'. In between making records she has hosted television shows and presented her own radio programmes, but times have not always been easy. She has operated a supermarket checkout, been a cloakroom attendant and worked as a waitress to earn money. 'You have to be prepared to take anything to keep going when things are tough,' she told me. 'You have to learn never to lose faith in yourself and to take the rough with the smooth.'

Journalism

Journalism is another overcrowded profession in which job security is certainly not what it was a few years ago. Probably the most important quality for a journalist to have is curiosity, followed by the skill to ask incisive questions and the ability to make a story different, to make it stand out in such a way that people will notice it.

If you are at school or college and are interested in journalism as a career, write as many articles as you can for the school or college magazine. Practice does make perfect. Work experience is vital, so volunteer to work unpaid during your holidays for the company you want to work for eventually. This will show the editor that you are really keen. It also gives you the opportunity to get involved, and if you do the job well, there is a good chance of a job if a suitable one comes along as people like to work with someone they know. If you have to earn money, then try to fit work experience around paid employment. If, for instance, you want to work on the radio and you are working in a supermarket during the day, offer to help out at your local radio station a couple of evenings a week, or at weekends. It is hard work, but it will pay off!

People such as Chris Evans and Emma Freud started this way. Vanessa Feltz began her journalistic career by researching thoroughly. She read everything she could get hold of to see what was missing. 'I wrote to some fairly obscure magazine and suggested an article on wedding flowers. I found an unusual slant, they liked it and printed it.' But beware of taking just any job in the hope that it will lead somewhere. Vanessa applied for a job as editorial assistant on *Campaign* magazine. She did not realize what the position actually involved. 'The editor told me to regard it as a springboard to wherever I wanted to go. I believed him, but I did not 'spring' anywhere. I worked hard and enthusiastically, but it was not the job for me and I got fired because I didn't look as though I enjoyed it!'

Book Publishing

The publishing industry has changed rapidly since the mid-1980s. Company mergers and acquisitions have created a few, very large publishing houses and reduced the number of small, independent publishers. What was once seen as a 'gentleman's' profession is now big business.

Jobs in book publishing include editorial, design, marketing, publicity and sales. The vast majority of people in publishing are female graduates, and most start at secretarial level and work their way up. Few publishing houses offer graduate training schemes.

If your aim is to be an editor, it helps if you have a degree or special interest in a particular area of publishing. The majority of graduates enter publishing with an English degree, but there are many types of publishing other than literary fiction. A qualification in biology or languages, for example, may help you secure an editorial post with a publisher of reference books. Commissioning editors, the people who think up ideas for books and sign up authors, need to have a great deal of commercial sense, an instinct for whether or not there is a market for the book out there. Bookselling experience can be invaluable for this type of role.

Compared to other media jobs, salaries are low in publishing. Fortunately, dress codes are fairly relaxed. For editorial, design, marketing and publicity jobs, staff are expected to look smart but not to dress formally. The more creative the job, the more liberal the dress code tends to be.

Public Relations and Advertising

Mark Borkowski runs a highly successful PR company in London. Like most employers in this industry, he is adamant that people working for him should not be seduced by the glamour. Mixing with the stars and entertaining the 'beautiful people' is only a small part of the job; discipline and attention to detail is vital when planning a successful campaign. 'Whether you are selling a product or a personality, you are selling a commodity,' Mark told me. 'You have to look at the commodity, look at the market and look at what you want to achieve.'

In this highly creative world, employers are looking for people with imagination, ideas and a certain flair, but the ability to work as part of the team is just as important. So many people want to work in this field that there is the temptation to try for any job in the hope that it will lead to the one you really want. This can happen in certain cases, but if your aim is to be a copywriter and there are few jobs around, do not apply for one as an account executive as the qualities needed are quite different.

Depending on the area of PR or advertising in which you work, you may have to think up ideas for campaigns, buy space in newspapers and magazines, design advertisements, write articles, co-ordinate radio and television commercials, organize promotional events or liaise with clients and attract new business. All these jobs require different capabilities. Formal qualifications vary. There are some good PR courses available at universities. Rita Rowe is joint Managing Director of Mason Williams, a PR agency in Manchester. She advises anyone thinking of taking a degree in PR to look for a sandwich course during which you spend a year working with an agency. Leeds, Sterling and Bournemouth universities, among others, offer sandwich courses. But qualifications alone will not necessarily get you the job.

'Two women came for interviews last week,' said Rita. 'Both had degrees in English and MBAs in PR. But the minute they walked through the door I knew I wouldn't employ them. The image was all wrong: they looked like a couple of first-year students! It didn't matter how bright they were; I knew they would not impress my clients.' You need poise, presence and personality for any job, and unless you are working as a print buyer, designer, artist or behind the scenes where you seldom meet the clients, you have to look the part. This may mean adopting a businesslike appearance or displaying flair and individuality. Either way, the image must be well thought through.

Qualities for Media Work

- total dedication
- motivation
- energy
- enthusiasm
- curiosity
- word-processing and computer skills
- organizational flair
- ability to work long hours
- ability to cope with the knocks
- observational skills
- ability to deal with people at all levels sensitively but firmly

Dress

- Be tidy.
- Make sure you are presenting a professional image.
- Be creative! It is a creative medium you are working in.
- If you are an actor, look the part!

POLITICS

In some senses, the public image of a politician, whether she be local or national, is the only image of a politician. This is because politicians perform work in public for the public. As a politician, you have a short-term contract that comes up for renewal every five years at the whim of members of the public. How you appear to the voters actually determines your future career.

The public image of politics has changed enormously over the last few years. A generation ago, that image was affected by the way in which politicians behaved in the House and how they handled debates or arguments. Most people formed their opinions through newspaper coverage of what was said in the Commons or their local council chamber, and through a few relatively respectful interviews on television and radio. Now we see politicians almost exclusively through radio and television. The Commons or the council chamber is no longer the fulcrum of debate, and what is said in the House gets very little coverage. Politics is covered by television and radio in a different way to newspapers. People get their news from radio and television, so newspapers have to provide something different, which is why they often go for the more sensational angle.

Of the message you put across on television, 83 per cent is visual and 17 per cent is aural. It is not so much what you say, but the way in which you say it! Giles Brandreth is MP for Chester. 'You have to be aware of how you come across. You may be opening the gates to paradise in what you're saying, but if you look tired, red-rimmed about the eyes, shifty, lacking in confidence with dandruff, that's what the viewers will remember!' His career as a journalist and television presenter has helped him. Being a familiar face, his image has made him more accessible. 'The star performers in any field of endeavour will tend to be individual, with a personality that is different but seems to ring true.' The old line 'once you can fake sincerity you've got it made' does not hold in politics anymore.

The Labour Party has been more conscious of its image of late, starting with the red rose campaign and the use of the name 'New Labour'. The party has actively encouraged women to become MPs. The life of an MP is, however, an arduous one, with late-night sittings, weeks spent at Westminster and horrendously busy weekends in the constituency.

To become involved in local politics, good local knowledge is essential. You also need to establish an image and woo the press because if nobody

knows about you, no one will vote for you. It is vital to show commitment. Go
to council meetings, read the local paper and get to know the party workers,
as they are the people who do the groundwork. A local selection committee
will certainly not be impressed by anyone who does not find out all she can
about the constituency she wants to represent.

Qualities
- commitment
- capacity for hard work
- excellent communication skills
- drive
- energy
- enthusiasm
- listening skills
- ability to work with people
- tenacity

Dress
It depends on the image you want to put across. Wearing a microskirt for a
visit to a factory might get you a substantial amount of press coverage, but it
could antagonize party workers! The three major political parties in Britain
today encourage their MPs to look professional, friendly and caring. So while
it is necessary to be smart, a hugely expensive designer suit would be
inappropriate on a visit round a sheltered housing unit.

THE HOTEL AND LEISURE INDUSTRY

A hotel's image is vital as it lives off its reputation. Although the image of
Holiday Inn hotels in the past was of fast food, chrome and plastic, the
acquisition of the Crown Plaza group gave them the high-quality image and
luxury end of the market they needed. Holiday Inn work hard to maintain the
positive image they have created for their hotels. How? There is a big
emphasis on staff training as they believe in investing in people; each room
has a comment card and visitors are encouraged to give their opinions on the
service and standards of the hotel; and there are two words printed on every
door that opens on to the public areas: 'On Stage'. In the hotel business you
are as much an actor as anyone treading the boards! However, the brave face

must be backed with sincerity. Most of the larger chains run incentive schemes and awards for staff who achieve high standards, and promotions are frequent, but Holiday Inn is the only hotel company to have a specific graduate training scheme that lasts one year.

To work in the hotel and leisure industry, good presentation and a professional image are vital, as well as the ability to stay and look cheerful after long hours on duty. The need to want to serve and help people is fundamental. If you cannot take orders cheerfully and with good grace, then this is not the area for you. The Ritz-Carlton Hotel Company has a chain of hotels in the USA and Australia. It has a specific self-image for their staff whose motto is 'We are Ladies and Gentlemen serving Ladies and Gentlemen'.

On another side of the leisure industry, Virgin Airlines builds on its innovative image which says value for money, quality products and fun. Will Whitehorn is Corporate Affairs Director for the Virgin Group. 'You can't create an image and sustain it for very long if it's not based on a foundation that is real.' In a high-risk, highly competitive business such as air travel, Virgin is flourishing. Its 'quality' image has helped build customer loyalty, which is the key to survival and success. Will told me: 'We have complaints from time to time. Planes are delayed, for instance, and things don't always work like clockwork. But when things go wrong we make sure we put them right as quickly as possible.' The reason Virgin has such a good image is word of mouth. It provides real value for money and the customers come back for more. Its staff are vitally important to maintaining that image. They are highly trained and, because so many people want to work for the company, Virgin can pick the cream of the crop. 'We want people who are intelligent, and who will be nice to people!' says Will.

Qualities
- tolerance
- understanding
- enthusiasm
- excellent communication skills
- willingness and ability to work long hours

Dress
In many large hotels, employees wear a uniform and have to look smart at all times. It promotes a sense of unity and equality amongst them. The staff at

the door and on reception are the first to greet the customers, so the image they create colours the way guests view the hotel as a whole. Holiday Inn have accounts with clothes companies to create a smart, classic look that will not date in a few years.

The same philosophy applies to airlines and many other sections of the leisure industry, whether the dress is tracksuits and trainers or a smart suit. If you are not provided with a uniform, a smart, professional appearance is what will be required.

CLERICAL WORK

Entry qualifications for clerical work vary depending on the company and the position for which you are applying. Generally, a good range of GCSEs and sometimes 'A' levels are required as well as a recognized secretarial qualification, such as Royal Society of Arts (RSA) level two in typing. Word-processing skills are essential, but shorthand is not used so much nowadays, although it can give you an advantage. You should aim for a typing speed of sixty to seventy words per minute. An understanding of telephone switchboards is advisable if you are doubling as a receptionist.

A good telephone manner is important, as you are often the first point of contact a customer has with a company. If you are worried that your voice might let you down, listen to it on a tape recorder – practise answering the phone and get used to how you sound to other people. (For more on the voice, *see Chapter 3*.) A cheerful, friendly personality is what employers want, as well as someone who can use her initiative. In all jobs you are working as part of a team, even if you are Personal Assistant to the Chief Executive, so the ability to work in harmony with others is vital. Someone who is moody and perverse can affect the morale of all those working with her, so do not take your problems to work!

There is an enormous diversity of clerical work. It can mean helping to entertain clients as well as supervising your boss's diary. Book-keeping, computer skills and a knowledge of languages can be a distinct advantage.

Qualities
- good communication skills
- ability to learn languages
- initiative

- computer skills
- enthusiasm
- tolerance

Dress

Take your lead from others in the office. Remember that bright colours stand out, which can be a good or a bad thing. Here are a few guidelines:

- Wear suits, jackets or smart shirts.
- Make sure that your skirts are not too short.
- Trousers should be smart if the organization permits them (some still do not!).
- Avoid sleeveless blouses.
- Have a good, clean pair of shoes.
- Keep your briefcase and handbag tidy.
- When meeting clients for the first time, or taking notes in board meetings, legs should be covered by tights or stockings, even if it is very hot.

SALES

To sell anything, an outgoing personality is important, but brashness is something that should be avoided at all costs. You need to look presentable and professional at all times because if people cannot believe in you they will not believe in your product, whatever it may be. Due to a tough marketplace, the status of the sales representative and sales assistant has grown over the last few years. The emphasis on sales is greater than ever before. You can produce the best product in the world, but if nobody sells it for you, your company will go bankrupt! More and more women are being recruited into selling, as their softer, more sympathetic approach is very effective. You do, however, have to have a pretty thick skin to cope with the rebuffs from all that cold calling.

If you cannot stand rejection, then think again before entering this tough world. It also requires long hours, often in the car, with sales areas sometimes stretching from Glasgow to Swindon. The rewards can be very high, so whether you are selling hi-fi equipment, double glazing, commodities, stocks and shares, clothes, ice cream or cars, this could be the job for you if you have 'the gift of the gab'!

Telesales

Telephone selling is very popular amongst woman with family commitments and also those who have taken early retirement. You need to like the job and love the phone! You also need to prepare yourself for the number of rejections you will receive and learn not to take them personally. Although you need to have drive and tenacity, you also have to be aware that companies receive hundreds of unsolicited calls, so tact and diplomacy is vital.

Qualities

- drive
- motivation
- ambition
- tact
- tenacity
- dedication
- enthusiasm
- ability to handle rejection
- good voice
- punctuality
- 'the gift of the gab!'

Dress

- If you have a uniform, make sure it is always clean and pressed.
- If you do not wear a uniform, a suit or jacket and skirt is appropriate dress.
- You should wear smart shoes and carry a briefcase.
- Keep a pair of driving shoes in the car, as nothing ruins your heels like driving.
- Take your jacket off when driving and lay it across the back seat of the car.
- Buy skirts in crease-resistant material.

Remember that in any field of work which puts you in front of the public, it is vital to create a positive image for you and your organization.

5

the interview

I have devoted this chapter to the interview because the aim of this book is primarily to help you create the positive image of yourself that is going to help you win that job or gain promotion. But handling yourself well in an interview might also help you achieve the position you want in a voluntary organization, get you elected to the board of governors of your children's school, become the chairperson of your golf club or be selected for the local council.

The information in this chapter should be relevant to anyone applying for a job, whether they be graduates or experienced employees looking for a new position. However, there is some specific advice for graduates at the end of the chapter.

Interviewers make up their mind about a candidate within the first sixty seconds of an interview. How you walk, how you say 'hello' and how you are dressed all help to form a positive or negative image. There are several things interviewers for any position will look out for:

- first impressions
- relevant experience
- necessary skills
- reason for applying
- preparation.

Recognized qualifications may be required for many careers, but for any post, the first impression must be a positive one. The number of applicants for most appointments is very high these days, so you only have a few minutes to make your mark and create a positive image. So what makes for a successful interview?

For many jobs you must look right and have a smart, businesslike appearance. As we have seen in the previous chapter, however, the way in which you dress for an interview should reflect the position you are seeking and the image of the organization. Preparation is all!

A successful interview will flow, and you will achieve a good rapport with your interviewer. A good, positive handshake is vital, but take your signal from the interviewer. Do not proffer a hand unless prompted, otherwise the interviewer may think you are trying to teach him or her manners. Eye contact is also important as we cannot tell what someone thinks or means unless we look into their eyes. They really are the window of the soul, so direct your gaze at the person who has asked you the question when you give your response; even if that person is busy writing notes, he or she is still listening to you. Listening skills are essential for you too; an interview can be thrown off course if you answer the question you thought you heard rather than the one that was asked. It sounds obvious, but it is surprising how many people (usually through nerves) rush into an answer. Listen not only to the question, but also to the question behind the question.

APPLYING FOR A JOB

A successful job application is one that is prepared thoroughly and well presented. Before sending off a job application, you should find out as much as you can about the job and the organization, and make sure your CV and covering letter are maximizing your chances of being asked to an interview.

First, find out the answers to the following questions about the organization to which you are applying:

- What does it do?
- Whom does it serve?
- Who owns it?
- What is its market?
- Who are the key personnel?

- How many people does it employ?
- What is its reputation?
- Is the annual turnover increasing or decreasing?

Armed with such information, your application can be more targeted, and should you be asked to an interview, you will already have a good deal of research about the company under your belt. This information can also help you to decide whether the company is one for which you really want to work.

Next, find out more about the job itself:

- What is the job title?
- What is its purpose?
- What are the terms and conditions?
- How will the job develop?

The company may have a brochure or formal job description it can send you to help you answer the above questions.

The Application Form

Some organizations will send you an application form which may be geared to the job. You should fill this in carefully and neatly. It can be useful to write out a rough version first. Unless otherwise specified, do not send any additional information, such as your CV or previous projects, with the application form.

The Curriculum Vitae

Your CV should not undersell or oversell you. There is no point in painting an unrealistic image of yourself on paper: it might get you an interview but, as soon as you walk in, the employer will know you are not right for the job.

Think of the vast number of CVs a prospective employer has to read through, and make sure yours is neat and to the point. If there are spelling mistakes, most people will immediately dismiss your application, unless you are the only relevant person for a particular job. Only use good-quality, white paper. People spend a fortune on coloured paper thinking it will help their application stand out, but when it comes through on a fax, it is often impossible to read.

Be careful what you put on your CV. Highlight the positive and diminish the negative. If you have three 'A' levels, for example, you should mention this on your CV and list the subjects, but if your grades were low it would be wise not to specify them. Draw attention to unusual features. If you have walked from John O'Groats to Land's End, say so. Do not just put 'walking' under your list of hobbies.

If you left school early without many qualifications, simply state the years you were in secondary education and then list the courses you have been on since. You might, for example, have been to night school and taken a word-processing course, an extra GCSE or learnt a language. You may have been sent on a presentation course and taken part in various training and development schemes at work. Make another list of 'transferable skills' learnt in your previous jobs. Managerial responsibilities, communication skills or something like organizing the firm's Christmas party all contribute to making you more attractive to a prospective employer. Even things like having your own telephone and a fax machine at home can seem very attractive to some employers if it means they can save money on providing them. The competition is so fierce these days that a determining factor could be something as simple as that.

Badly presented CVs:
- will be on cheap or coloured paper
- will have an indistinct typeface
- will list the most recent job last
- will not highlight unusual features
- will give too much irrelevant personal detail, such as 'I have three goldfish and four cats' or 'I am captain of the bridge club and play at least three evenings a week' (this might suggest that you would not want to work overtime).

Well-presented CVs:
- contain no spelling errors
- are short, sharp and to the point (covering not more than two A4 pages)
- are on good-quality, white paper
- have a clear, attractive typeface.

Many personnel people spend no longer than six seconds glancing at a CV so it must be well presented. If possible, it should be typed on a word processor and printed on a high-quality printer.

Age

Should you state your date of birth on your CV? Some companies specify an age range in their job advertisements. This practice can, however, backfire. If, for example, the given age range is 28–36, an ideal candidate aged 37 might be deterred from applying. Before you respond to such an advertisement, ask yourself whether this is the sort of company for which you want to work.

If you are older than the top of the specified age range but think you are right for the job, write a really stunning letter to accompany your CV and do not mention your age. Once you get an interview you can make up your mind whether to mention it or not. If you are right for the job, it should not make a difference. Do not lie about your age, however, as it might raise doubts about your honesty in other areas.

Even when employers do not specify an age range, age is still a thorny issue for the job applicant. If you put your date of birth on your CV, a prospective employer will make instant perceptions from it. Age should be a secondary thing, so if you are in doubt, skip it and sell your skills, qualities and qualifications.

Hobbies and Interests

Most people mention their hobbies and interests outside work on their CV. This is a useful way of indicating something about your personality to the employer before the interview and to show that you are a sociable, well-rounded individual. However, you should be careful that what you include is relevant and shows you in a positive light.

Hobbies, sports and previous experience are all important if they add value to the job you are seeking. Involvement in amateur dramatics or being the chairperson of the debating society at university would be relevant to include on your CV if you were applying for a job in sales or teaching, for example, whereas it would not help if you wanted to be a computer programmer. If you are captain of the squash team it probably means you are good with people, but too much activity might imply that you have not had time to concentrate fully on your work. Be careful how you word things.

Try and put yourself in the employer's position as much as possible. The company is looking for transferable skills that have been gained from a number of different activities. It is not just the fact that you joined the basketball team or were part of a research group that is relevant, but how you contributed. If you cannot give an indication of what these transferable skills are, then in an employer's eyes, you have gained nothing. A good example of learning from experience might read: 'We were on a losing streak and I found morale was getting low. I discussed this with a couple of colleagues and we decided on a new tack which helped us win the next few games/move the project forward.'

The Covering Letter

You should write a covering letter to accompany your CV or application form. The covering letter should be addressed to the person who invited the application and targeted to the organization. A generic covering letter will put most prospective employers off, but one that mentions why you are keen to work for their company would be viewed positively. Use the covering letter as an opportunity to highlight the skills and experience that are relevant to that job. Again, correct spelling is crucial, particularly of the name of the company and the person you are addressing.

Here is an example of a good covering letter:

Dear Mr Green

With reference to your recent advertisement in *The Echo* for an Administrator, I read with interest that you are looking for applicants with good communication skills. I have enclosed my CV, and would like to highlight the fact that I have spent the last five years co-ordinating tours for our Youth Band. As some of the tours were in Germany and Holland, I had to use my language skills. As well as organizing insurance, travel arrangements and hostel accommodation, I had to deal with seasick trumpet players, homesick banjo players and a double bass that went missing. I feel this has given me an insight into financial services and helped me enormously in my dealings with people.

I very much look forward to meeting you.

Yours sincerely

Graphology

Nobody is employed by a Swiss bank or by Air France, whether as a cleaner or a pilot, without a graphology or handwriting test. Job advertisements often ask for applications to be handwritten. We tend to think that an application form is only acceptable if it is on the word processor, but graphology is becoming more popular in Europe. Although these tests are not necessarily accurate, they are likely to be used more and more, so forewarned is forearmed! If, however, a job advertisement does not specify that applications should be handwritten, it is better to type your covering letter.

THE INTERVIEW

Preparation is the key to confidence and confidence is the key to success! Before the interview, find out as much as you can: who the interviewer is, his or her role in the recruitment process and how long the interview is likely to take. Lana Jeffers is Director of Middleton Jeffers Recruitment Ltd. in London. She told me: 'Because there are so few jobs now, people must make a real effort. If you want to work in the city you must read the *Financial Times* every day. If you want to work in advertising you must read *Campaign* every week. You must convince a prospective employer that you are interested in the industry. It is a total waste of their time to train you for six months only to find that you don't like the job after all.'

To Lana Jeffers, like many recruitment agents, references are very important, and she always checks them thoroughly before sending anyone to an interview. You should give the name, address and telephone number of two referees on your CV, making sure you obtain their permission first. A previous employer is ideal, provided that you were happy in the job, and that some of the same skills are needed in the post for which you are applying. If you do not wish your current employer to know that you are applying for another job, do not give his or her name as a referee. If an interviewer questions this, be honest and say that you do not want to mention your application to your employer at this stage.

Apart from former employers, the best referees are people in a responsible position, such as your accountant or solicitor, or family friends who have known you for a reasonable length of time. It is not advisable to ask members of your immediate family to provide references. If, however, you have been working for a family business, the referee should state the relationship and write the reference in an unbiased way.

How else can you prepare for an interview? Do not leave it too late – by the time you are panicking it is too late! Always be positive – you will not be offered a job if you do not believe in yourself. Despite the high numbers of applicants, most companies are still hard pressed to fill places with the right people, so they look hard at anyone with potential.

Spend some time thinking about yourself. Write down three adjectives that you would like somebody to use to describe you after a first meeting. One might be 'enthusiastic'; if so, make sure this side of your personality comes across in your interview. 'Hardworking' might be another; if so, show evidence of a project that you have worked on. Write down other characteristics and see if they match up to the job description.

If you would describe yourself as very ambitious, a small business might not have the scope for expansion and promotion that you are looking for. Make a note to ask questions at the interview about career progression. Write down your strengths and weaknesses and consider them carefully. Can the weaknesses be improved upon, and if so, how?

Dressing for the Interview

It is a sign of disrespect for the interviewer if you do not make an effort to look your best. Even though the interviewer will be aware that you are dressing to impress, the signal you are giving is 'I respect you and your status as an interviewer, and I am reflecting that in what I'm wearing'.

What you wear to an interview depends on the type of job for which you are applying. People who work in the media often dress less formally than those in the legal profession, for example. To find out how people dress at the company to which you have applied, you could wait outside the offices at home time or go to a pub where employees of that firm might congregate after work. In some careers, such as social work, casual dressing is acceptable because it is the best way to associate with clients. However, you should still wear something smart for a job interview.

Mary Spillane is the founder of the image consultancy firm 'Color Me Beautiful'. Before coming to Britain she worked in government and public policy in the USA, as well as in journalism and PR. She felt, as an American, that the British were very different, especially in the field of presentation. She told me: 'This self-denying approach that the British took was charming in Britain, but it didn't travel well in the modern world. Americans are very visual people; they rely far more on visual information than they do on the written word.'

The 'packaging' of people and their image is very important. If you look tired and slightly unwell, your prospective employer might doubt your ability to work hard and do the job properly. Colour is crucial, as it can help you to look confident and healthy, reinforcing the fact that you have the stamina and ability to do the job. Colours also make a statement about your personality, but for interviews it is best to wear neutral colours. If you wear shocking pink, the interviewer may think that you are disruptive or aggressive. Alternatively, it might be viewed more positively, in that you are likely to stand out and make your mark. It depends on the nature of the organization, so do your homework!

Everybody is different, so it is important to find out what suits you. Employers are not looking for clones; they want something individual. Individuals contribute; they offer that little bit extra that every company is looking for. You can make a fairly formal outfit look individual by adding accessories such as a pair of handmade earrings or an unusual belt, brooch or scarf, but beware of too much jewellery.

Comfort is essential. If you are uncomfortable during the interview you will not perform at your best. 'I'd like men to wear a skirted suit and heels and sheer tights,' declares Mary Spillane 'and then try and put in twelve- or thirteen-hour days!' The importance of comfort does not, however, give you an excuse to 'slob out' or wear any shoes to death because they are so comfy. The ones you wear for your interview must be clean and smart. The golden rule is to make sure that you can run down the street in your clothes, that they button easily so that the body can work, and that you are able to eat without them feeling too tight!

For most interviews it is appropriate to wear a skirt and jacket. Save the smart trousers for when you have got the job. If the weather is very hot, try to find something that is cool and comfortable but smart. Skimpy tops are a definite 'no-no' unless you are going to keep the jacket on all the time, and even then there should be no plunging necklines. See-through shirts ought to have a vest top underneath, not just a bra. Sleeveless blouses should have straps at least two inches wide, but short or capped sleeves generally look more appropriate. Shiny material for dresses is out, as are peep-toe shoes. It is generally recognized that a dress does not look as professional as a skirt and jacket, and that sundresses are not professional at all! There is a school of thought that says pastel shades and floral blouses are not as credible as plain, darker colours, but in my view, you do not need to dress like a man to compete with him.

Some people would say that you should never show toes at work, but in very hot weather, sandals worn without tights are acceptable these days, and court shoes with low heels or slingbacks are always suitable. I hate wearing tights in the summer, but a sheer, light pair of tights or stockings do finish off an outfit and make you look and feel more professional. They should be worn at an interview or any important meeting. Always make sure they are unladdered and smooth!

You should be able to wear your 'interview suit' both at work and socially. If you are going to wear light-coloured suits and jackets regularly, it is a good idea to ensure they do not have to be dry-cleaned as this is both impractical and expensive. Always try and choose fabrics that will look smart and classy with the minimum amount of care.

There is no point spending a lot of money on a beautiful outfit if nobody is going to notice your face, so make-up is very important. Worse than no make-up, however, is too much – the heavy dark eyes or the fuchsia lips. Make-up should complete the 'look' so that you seem well groomed, well polished and fresh. (For more advice on making the most of your face, *see* Chapter 1.

The Weekend Interview

Some interviews are held at weekends. These are generally residential and often include a variety of activities, some of them outdoors, to try and find out as much about you as possible. If you are asked to attend such an interview, a suit would probably be too formal. So, what should you wear?

Knowing how to dress down is just as critical as knowing how to dress up. Do not assume that you can get away with your own notion of what is casual. In Mary Spillane's view 'a jacket is for a woman the extra layer of armour she always needs. If she only has one layer, the blouse or the little top of some sort, she is vulnerable and won't have any status'. A jacket gives you status, and you can always take it off if you want to. A casual jacket can be colourful but not scruffy.

Do not wear your favourite Doc Martens if they have seen better days; a flat shoe, with perhaps a little detail, is a good idea. Trousers or jeans are fine if they are reasonably smart, especially when finished off with a jacket. This type of dress would also be suitable for any training courses you may be sent on. It always amazes me that some women think they can wear whatever they like to courses where the dress is 'casual', even shorts and see-through blouses. It would not be so bad if they had the figures to wear them! Whenever you are representing your organization, look the part – you never know who is going to be there.

There is a trend in some companies to encourage staff to wear casual clothes on Fridays. This can be a double-edged sword. Although it gives you the chance to show your personality, your dress can let you down. Remember that you may suddenly have to visit a client or attend an emergency board meeting. But smart leggings and a designer T-shirt or sweater would be suitable, or a skirt and jumper rather than a jacket. If in doubt, play safe.

Remember the following points about dressing for an interview:

- Each job sector has a personality and a culture.
- Learn about the culture.
- Find out what suits you.
- Find out what colours help you to look as fit and healthy as possible.
- Have some personality in your clothes.
- Dress appropriately.
- Comfort is essential. If you are not comfortable you cannot perform properly.
- Buy good, interesting accessories.

Interview Techniques

Interviewing techniques vary from company to company. You could be interviewed one-to-one, by a panel or board or by two people. All three techniques have advantages and disadvantages. If there is only one person interviewing you, then his or her likes and dislikes, moods and prejudices have to be taken into account. The panel may be rather intimidating, as can being interviewed by two people who adopt opposite roles to see what reaction they get. This type of interview is often conducted by a man and a woman. The woman usually takes the sympathetic role and tries to put the candidate at her ease, drawing out more information. The man plays devil's advocate and can be quite aggressive to see how the interviewee reacts under stress and how she copes with widely varying behaviour.

Sometimes the people conducting the interview are not properly trained, and this can be an uncomfortable experience. If the interviewer is playing a power game, keep your cool and remember that it is not personal. Another sign of an untrained or inexperienced interviewer is one who asks closed or leading questions in a rather haphazard way, frequently interrupting. Other poor interviewers may do all the talking, not allowing you to get your points across. In such instances, it is difficult to be assertive and make your point without seeming aggressive. If you are frequently interrupted, use phrases such as: 'Could I just go back to ...', 'From past experience I have found ...', 'May I clarify a point you made earlier, because it seems to me that ...'. Keep talking enthusiastically so that your interviewer does not have the chance to jump in until you have finished what you want to say.

A good interviewer should start the interview on time and have your details lying on the desk in front of him or her. He or she should ask open questions that allow you to expand to include the points you want to get across. There is also the 'halo and horns' syndrome to be taken into account: we tend to warm to people who share our own values and views, but good interviewers should be aware of this and disregard it as much as possible. Some interviewers take notes, but if they do not it does not mean that you are so boring there is nothing to write about!

Do not lose heart if you are interviewed badly and do not get offered the job. Did you really want to work for that person anyway? Every interview, good or bad, is useful experience. It is a good idea to write down the type of questions you were asked and the reactions to your answers; you can refer to this record when you go for your next interview.

Making a Good Impression

For any interview it is essential to walk in like a winner and put across a very positive image. You have to give of your best, and show the interviewer the most compelling facets of yourself. In the final analysis, it is not necessarily qualifications that will win you the position you want, but personal chemistry and image. When you arrive, chat to the receptionist, and ascertain where the interview will take place. Check your appearance; you do not want lipstick on your teeth or a label sticking out of your jacket. Think about what you will say to the interviewer when you meet, and mentally revise the research about the company you have done and think about the qualities needed for the job.

If you are shown up to the room where the interviews are being held, try and make small talk with whomever accompanies you, even if it is only about the weather. You never know what questions could be put to the staff to elicit information about you afterwards. A conversation, however trivial, will also help you to relax and loosen up your voice. When you get into the room, sit up straight in the chair and look alert! Most important of all, be yourself, not what you think someone wants you to be.

Take a good-quality notepad and pen into the interview so that you can make notes if you feel it useful. Making a few notes also impresses many prospective employers, as it shows you are taking a real interest. You may also find it helpful to have made some notes in advance to take to the interview. If your mind goes blank, headings help to jog the memory. Jot down any evidence of how you fulfil specific criteria specified in the advertisement. Think of the questions you want to ask and make a note of them, but do not feel obliged to ask something. It is fine to say, 'Thank you very much, but I think you have covered everything I need to know'.

The way in which you handle the interview is very important. This is particularly the case when applying for a different job in the same company as, however well the interviewer may know you, you will not get the job if your interview technique is poor. It helps if you treat the interviewer as if he or she had never met you before, and do not assume that they know certain things about you.

Interview Questions

There are many types of interview question. Some questions are straight-forward, others potentially more tricky. If you are asked a difficult question that picks up something negative on your CV, do not panic. Stay calm, be reasonably honest and accent the positive. For example, if one of the questions asked is 'Why have you got such a poor degree when your "A" level results were so good?', the answer might be 'I got to university and discovered non-stop partying, but now I've learnt my lesson'. At least you are showing that you are being honest and have gained something from the experience.

Experience can mean different things to different people, and it is something that is often addressed by interviewers. Someone who has been in a managerial position for eighteen months may be just as capable as someone who has been in the same position for five years. In fact, the former may be better suited, as there is a law of diminishing returns after a certain length of time in a job. If you have been in a job for a significant period, it is important to say why you have stayed and what both you and the company have gained as a result; then say why you are leaving.

Here are some examples of the different types of interview questions you may be asked:

Closed Questions

These are the most difficult questions to answer as they are not designed to allow you to elaborate. They are usually phrased thus:

- Did you...
- Who was...
- Which company...

Leading Questions

These prompt a short or particular answer. Examples include:

- Do you think you...
- Can you...
- Are you...

Open Questions

These allow you the most scope in your answer:

- Why did you...
- When were you...
- Where have you...
- How did you...

Open questions are the ideal, but if you think you are being interviewed by somebody who is not bringing out the best in you, answer the closed or leading question as if it were an open one. You might, for example, be asked 'Do you think you have initiative?'. Instead of answering 'yes' or 'no', you could give an example of when you have shown this quality in the past, such as 'I do think I have initiative because last year, when we had a small fire in the office, people started to panic, so I sounded the alarm, told someone to ring the fire brigade and then made sure everyone was evacuated quickly and quietly'. Or if you were asked 'Are you willing to travel with this job?', the answer could be 'Yes. I have travelled a lot ever since being at school and always enjoyed the challenge of meeting new people and seeing new places'.

Hypothetical Questions

These are usually phrased as follows:

- What would you do if...
- How would you tackle...
- Supposing that...

Try and answer these questions as honestly as you can and imagine what the ideal employee would do, taking into account the job description.

Questions to Expect

Here are some examples of common interview questions with some ideal answers which you may be able to tailor to your requirements.

> *Summarize the skills and knowledge you have gained.*
> As senior sales assistant I had to deal with all kinds of queries, from staff as well as customers. I also had to make sure the goods were displayed properly, handle the accounts and, most useful of all, learn to negotiate with suppliers.

> Or
> As a secretary at Sanders and Gupta I had to act as receptionist too. This meant speaking to clients and answering their more simple queries. It has given me a lot of responsibility and helped me in my dealings with people.

> *What would you consider as adequate reward for your efforts?*
> (This sort of question is to test you and learn more about your personality. If you have already found out what the salary is, quote that figure. If the company has not mentioned the salary, talk to friends in similar situations

and look at other job advertisements to get an idea of the sort of figure you should be expecting.)

I would naturally like to be paid the going rate for my services! But more than that, I would want the chance to develop my skills as a manager and expand my knowledge of the industry.

What are your strengths?
(Here you have the chance to talk about the good points that might be listed on your CV.)

As you can see, I have had several jobs in the holidays that have helped me understand how a retail outlet works. I also had to organize people's travel arrangements when I was captain of the hockey team, so I feel I have both the personality and the experience needed to work in the travel industry.

Or
I have spent the last two years running the sales team, and as the product we were selling was new to the market, it meant that I had to look at new outlets, and also to motivate the staff, who were a little unsure of the strategy to begin with.

Would you say you have any weaknesses?

Yes. I would say that I am a perfectionist.

Or
Yes. I think I am very demanding, and I expect a lot from myself.

What has been your biggest accomplishment?
(Think of something that you are proud of, either at work, school, college or in sport, but make it work-related.)

I won the Southwest Inter-Schools Public Speaking Prize in my last year at school.

Or
At my last company I helped organize a raffle to raise money for
charity. We made over £500, twice as much as had been raised
before.

Tell me how you moved up through the organization?
I worked hard and really thought about where I wanted to go. I was
also fortunate that at a time when Kidman's was expanding, I was in
a position to head up a new department.

Why have you had so many jobs?
Well, after I had been at Wren's for a year, they had to make
redundancies. As I was the last in, I'm afraid I was first out. It was
the same at Charlton's. To be honest, I think I accepted my present
job without thinking it through first. The job wasn't right for me as it
offered no chance of promotion, so I thought it was better to try and
find something that would use my particular skills more fully.

Why were you dismissed?
I wanted a position which would provide opportunities to develop
my career but I found that trying for greater responsibility created
conflict. As you know, job searching takes a lot of time, so it was
thought best (by both me and the company) that I should have the
time to concentrate on finding the right job.

You see this clock on the desk? Sell it to me.
(This question might be asked at an interview for a sales position.)

What is special about this clock? Apart from the obvious quality of
the design, its battery is guaranteed for three years; it has a large,
luminous dial so that it can be seen easily in the dark (ideal for an
older person); and it is on special offer – a third off its usual price –
which makes it just £9.99 until the end of the month.

What sort of sport do you like?
(This is asked partly to see if you are a team player, but also to see whether
the sport might interfere with your work.)

I like to keep myself fit, so I play tennis at least once a week.

Or
I am a member of the local rowing club. We take part in a number
of competitions, but I make sure there is always a substitute, as I
would hate to let them down if I am working away.

What are your hobbies?
(This question is usually asked to find out more about you, and as physical
and mental health is high on any employer's mind the answer might be:)

I like gardening. It helps me relax and often provides valuable
thinking time if I need it. It also keeps me fit.

Or
I enjoy cooking. I pick up recipes from different countries. It has
really broadened my horizons.

(Both these answers tell the interviewer something positive about you.
Whatever you do as a hobby, try to relate it to the job you are going for. If the
job on offer means plenty of foreign travel and your hobby is cooking, the
above answer would tell the prospective employer that you would feel at
home entertaining clients in different countries.)

How do you organize and plan major projects?
(A tricky one!)

First, I would establish what the key objectives are, when the
project has to be finished and how much money is involved. How I
would proceed would depend on the nature of the project.

Have you ever had any financial difficulties?
(Another tricky one, but be as honest as you can.)

Nothing my bank manager and I can't cope with!
Or

Yes. I had a problem last year which has now been resolved. As a
result of that I have...

Describe a difficult problem that you have solved.
(If you are a graduate or going for your first job, use an example from
college, school or home. If you are working, think of a problem you have
resolved recently. It does not have to be a major one. The interviewer wants
to see whether you use your initiative and can handle the bad times as well
as the good.)

We found we had a problem with one line of goods. I rang those
particular customers to apologize, and made sure they got
replacement deliveries as soon as possible.

Where do you see yourself in five years' time?
Or
How long will you stay with the company if you get the job?

I want to be here on a long-term basis. As far as I can see, there are
many opportunities, and as you seem to reward progress, I hope to
be able to learn the job and climb the ladder as other positions and
opportunities arise.

*There must have been times when you and your manager disagreed.
Why?*
Here the interviewer is trying to find out if you are difficult to work with.
Unless you had regular rows, the answer might be:

I can't think of a time when we really disagreed. He/she was very
good in that he/she would let me have my say, but we always got
on well.

Which aspects of the job description for this position do you dislike?
Or
What are your dislikes?
(The first question is specifically about the job. Having done your homework,
you will know what the job entails. Make it the more mundane things that do

not appeal. The second question is more general, but angle your general
dislikes to the job too, as well as things like television soaps or whatever
they might be. Have a reason for disliking anything, but do not go into a
long tirade!)

> Filing and photocopying aren't my favourite occupations! But I know
> that it is all part of the job, and I never mind doing anything that has
> a purpose to it.

> Or
> I don't like *Eastenders* because, although I appreciate it is trying to
> mirror life, the story lines are a bit too gloomy!

> *Why should I take you on? Why do you think you will be good at the job?*

> I think I have the right blend of experience and drive that will make
> both me and the company successful.

(Then substantiate the statement with experience.)

> *You only got a ' C ' in English Literature GCSE. Were you satisfied with that?*

> I only decided to take the exam at the last minute, so I didn't have as
> much time to revise as I would have liked. However, it has given me
> an interest in literature as a whole, and I find I read a lot more now.

Personal Questions

Personal questions can be off-putting and even offensive. If interviewers
want to know too much about your personal life, do you really want to work
for them? 'Why aren't you married?' is none of their business, and 'Are you
thinking of getting married?' is only really applicable if you are applying to
run a pub or to become a vicar, where the parishioners may prefer a married
priest.

'Do you intend to have children?' is not a politically correct question
these days, even though an employer might be trying to find out how long
you intend to stay in the job. The answer to these questions would be 'I do
not think that has any bearing on my ability to do the job'. This must be said
pleasantly and with a smile. Move on quickly to another point.

Some years ago, I was interviewed by a television company and was asked 'What will you do when your children are ill?'. My reply was 'I have applied for the job because I really want to work for Central Television and believe I will be good at reading the news. My domestic arrangements are my responsibility and will not interfere with my work'. I got the job! The answer to 'Do you have children?' depends on the job. If you are going to work with children, write about them or sell children's toys, this would be an advantage. If you do not have children of your own, mention nephews or nieces and any godchildren.

Never get involved in an argument with a prospective employer, even if you feel severely provoked. The interviewer will be testing you to see how well you react to confrontation and stress. There is no need to show your intellectual abilities by lecturing your interviewer, and avoid being critical of previous employers, as it does not show you in a good light.

Tests

Some companies, such as IBM, ask interview candidates to sit psychometric tests. These are designed to find out more about you and determine whether you are suitable for the job for which you are applying. Some firms also carry out spelling and numeracy tests and use graphology (*see page 82*). Personality tests are becoming more important, but they are very expensive to administer. The Occupational Preference Questionnaire (OPQ) asks job-related questions to select the ideal candidate for the position.

Psychometric tests will help define people fairly accurately. The sort of questions used in the tests might be:

- Do you get angry easily?
- Do you prefer to read a book or watch television?
- If there is conflict do you move away quickly?

The tests have a built-in lie detector but there is no right or wrong answer. We all fit into a category, and some people have different strengths for different jobs. The tests are meant to help, so do not be intimidated by them.

Telephone Interviews

Some organizations employ companies to sift through applicants by conducting the first interview over the phone. As you may not be given advance warning of the interview, be prepared. Have any notes near the phone when you start the interview, but make sure the desk or table is clear. It is so easy to be distracted and you need to concentrate harder when there is nobody to focus on. Keep the following guidelines in mind:

- Do not be overfamiliar with the interviewer.
- Avoid 'yes' or 'no' answers. Try to elaborate on closed questions (*see page 89*).
- Be brief but factual.
- Ask questions.
- Take notes, if not during the call, then as soon as you put the phone down.

Telephone conversations are a skill. Here are some techniques you can adopt to ensure you are coming across well. Some of them apply to telephone interviews, and others are more general.

- Listen attentively. The ear you use makes a difference. Use the right ear when absorbing complicated information. This is because it connects with the logical side of the brain (the left side). Use the left ear when listening sympathetically, as it connects with the more imaginative right side of the brain.
- Listen to the call with your full attention, and try to smile when you speak.
- If you are expecting a difficult call, take the initiative where possible and make contact first. Get to the point quickly: 'The reason I have called you is because...'.
- If you are caught on the hop by a call or feel unprepared, 'stall but call' – call back after checking any relevant facts and information. This will also give yourself time to think.
- When dealing with complaints, do not take them too personally, keep calm, allow the caller to voice all his or her complaints without interruption, and listen sympathetically.
- If you are complaining, decide first what you want to achieve from the call, such as a refund, an apology or replacement of goods. Never lose your temper!
- If the phone rings when you have a visitor, either at home or in the office, tell the caller politely that you will ring him or her back. If it is

urgent, make the call as brief as possible, and either leave the room, or gesture to your guest that you will not be long.

■ Never ask a customer or client to ring back. If someone has taken the trouble to contact you, then you or your boss should return the call. Business has been lost through this slight portrayal of bad manners!

■ Find out and use the caller's name and take relevant details as you talk.

CAREERS ADVISORY SERVICES

Robin Wood is Chief Executive of Career Movers Companion, a recruitment and advisory company with offices in the northwest of England and in Reading. He helps graduates, people in work and those who have been made redundant to find jobs. Once more, it all comes down to preparation. If graduates come to him with no idea of what they want to do, they are given a psychometric test to identify areas and occupations to which they are likely to be most suited. Then the job of writing the CV and a good covering letter is followed by the search for suitable companies for those graduates to approach.

In Robin's experience, unsolicited CVs accompanied by carefully constructed letters are very successful because there is not the same competition as when a job has been advertised on the open market. There are plenty of jobs around, but you may find that some previously done by non-graduates will be filled by graduates, so be prepared to lower your sights a bit.

For people in their forties and fifties who have been made redundant, the future is brighter than it was a couple of years ago. In 1995, Career Movers Companion found positions for more people in the forty-eight to fifty-three age bracket than ever before. 'There seems to be a move away from the twenty-eight to thirty-year-old who is all whiz kid and MBA,' says Robin. 'Many companies now recognize the value of experience, and there is a feeling that if someone has done a particular job well for three companies, she will work well for you too.' Redundancy is traumatizing even if there has been a substantial payoff, so the effort to re-create a positive image can be hard. When you are in the pit, at the bottom of the Transition Curve, it can be difficult to climb out. Self-motivation is vital, and the most important thing for more mature applicants is to identify transferable skills from the job they have left to organizations where those skills will provide added value. Comprehensive research is essential.

The cost of using a careers advisory service varies, but it will probably be in the region of £350–£500. Some companies charge much more, so ask around. The best recommendation is from somebody who has used the firm successfully. The fee includes constructing the CV, writing letters, researching companies, brushing up on interview skills and, in many cases, counselling. It takes about four and a half months for most people to be 'placed'.

GRADUATES

Not all undergraduates make the most of their Careers Advisory Service (CAS) at university or college. The CAS is staffed by professionals who work closely with many companies. They can offer help and guidance to undergraduates, such as sending them on workshops to improve their interviewing skills.

Many companies visit universities in what is known as the 'milk round'. The first visit is likely to be to a careers fair, where undergraduates are encouraged to ask questions from company reps and find out more information about the company before applying. Interviews then take place before final examinations. If you interview well and are offered a job, it will usually be conditional on the grade of degree you achieve, although you will always be expected to get the best classification of degree you can.

David Thomas is Head of Development and Training supply at BT. From the huge numbers of applications that come in, relatively few are selected for interview. 'We had a woman in last week who thought she had a reasonable chance, but during the interview she spoke in a monotone and spent the whole time looking at her knees. When I asked her at the end how she would describe herself, she looked at me and said 'My friends would say I am bright and cheery'. Interviewers want your personality to come across during an interview. If you say you are bright and cheery, then there must be evidence to suggest that you are!

The standard question from students is 'Can you tell me more about the company's training and development policy?'. If, however, you can ask a question that shows that you have thoroughly researched the company, that will make a much greater impression on the interviewer. For a company such as BT, a good question might be 'My interest is software engineering. Is that likely to be stimulated by the multimedia work that BT is doing?'. This shows an understanding of the nature of the business. The more specific you are, the more profitable the line of interview will be, as it indicates a focus on the part of the applicant.

It is also important to be well informed, both in terms of current affairs and about the industry in which you are interested. Read trade magazines and try to take a newspaper every day, preferably a broadsheet. The tabloids might run a story about BT, for example, with the shock headline 'Granny cut off in the Highlands', whereas the broadsheets would give you more information. When you are asked at interview 'What do you know about the company?', you might answer 'I was very surprised to learn how restricted BT's licence was when it comes to multimedia provision to people's homes'.

As well as being interviewed, undergraduate job applicants might be also asked to carry out an exercise. Someone applying for a researcher's job with a broadcasting company might be asked to write a programme proposal, for example. Role-play is something the BBC has introduced. One scenario during an interview for a production secretary went like this: during an important production meeting for Religious Programmes, the editor specified that on no account did he want to be disturbed, unless it was by the Director General himself. The production secretary's job was to keep people out. A senior producer rushed in to say that she had managed to fix an interview with the Pope, but needed the go-ahead immediately if this fantastic opportunity was not to be missed. She was very insistent, and most of the applicants, swayed by her powerful argument and aggressive attitude, let her in. The correct response would have been to tell her politely that you had been told under no circumstances to interrupt the meeting, and that it was not your job to make editorial decisions about the programme, therefore she would have to wait until the meeting finished before speaking to the editor. A production secretary is not paid to make those sort of heavyweight judgements!

Again, preparation is all. If you are applying to work on a specific programme in any capacity, whether at the BBC or with another broadcasting company, it is vital to have a critical appraisal about it. But be constructive in your criticism, as you have to be conscious that the series editor may be present.

Royal Insurance has put together a profile of the type of graduate that fits into the organization. This was based on previous years' experience of selecting interviewees from the many CVs that arrive at their office in Liverpool. They told me, 'We now look for someone with an upper-second degree, with work experience; someone who can work in a team and has been involved with people both in and out of university.' Someone with no interest outside their academic studies and/or no work experience would be precluded by many companies. It is also necessary to understand the relevance of a degree to the work you are seeking; just to have gone to school and then to university is not enough.

SUMMARY

Preparing for the Interview
- Remember – the first process is rejection, the second is selection.
- Know what you are applying for.
- Do not send any projects or proof of work unless requested to do so.
- Fill in application forms properly – do not just put 'refer to CV'.
- Find out as much as possible about the organization and what it does. Use the library, read relevant magazines or ring the personnel department to find out more.
- If information is not forthcoming, demonstrate that you have tried to find it.
- Talk to people who work in that industry to find out what the job entails.
- Find out what makes a person successful in that job.
- Use as many contacts as you can.
- Be honest in your CV – don't build up your experience as the interviewer will see through it.
- Make sure your CV is well presented.
- Have an early night before the interview!

Mistakes to Avoid
- Bad spelling and other errors on CVs.
- Being late.
- Not being alert.
- Not asking intelligent questions.
- Not thinking things through.
- Lack of preparation.

Appearance and Presentation
- If the outfit is fairly cheap, spend money on shoes, handbag or briefcase.
- Do not wear too much jewellery.

- Wear some make-up, but not too much.
- Be well manicured but avoid very bright nail polish.
- Do not carry too many bags.
- Be aware of your body language and voice.
- Do not be too loud or pushy.
- Give a firm handshake.
- Create and maintain eye contact.
- Be enthusiastic!

6

giving a presentation

Most of us will have to give a presentation or make a speech at some
time in our lives. It may be to a handful of colleagues or to an audience of
thousands. Whether you are addressing a local charity committee or a
business seminar, the ability to put your point across in an interesting and
informative way is essential. In today's competitive business world, the
woman who can communicate with authority and confidence has a great
advantage over her peers. If you are asked to speak at a social function, then
you are quite within your rights to decline if you want to, but if it is part of
your job, you have no choice. Today, making presentations is a part of most
people's working lives. It is vitally important to do them well, and those who
are good communicators are the ones who will make it to the top.

INITIAL QUESTIONS

Thorough preparation is, again, the key to confidence which, in turn, is
the key to success. In order to be able to prepare, there are a number of
questions you need to ask yourself before you accept the invitation to speak:

1 Why have they asked me?
2 Whom will I be addressing and how large will the audience be?
3 Where will the presentation/speech take place?
4 For how long should the presentation/speech last?
5 Are there any other speakers?

1. Why You?

You will be asked to speak for a number of reasons. It may be because you are a good raconteur or because you are the expert in that field. The fact that you have been asked to speak should give you confidence. If you are an expert in the area, you probably will not have to do as much research for your presentation.

2. The Audience

Every speech, talk or presentation should be written with the audience in mind. What does the audience want or need to hear? It sounds an obvious point to make, but it is surprising how many people stand up and say what *they* want to say, not what the audience needs to hear! Find out in advance the age group of the audience, whether it is going to be mostly male or female, and the job categories of the audience members. All this information will help you target your presentation appropriately. You will also need to take into consideration the size of the audience. If you are addressing a hall full of people, your tone would probably need to be more formal than with a small group.

3. The Venue

In order to plan your journey, you need to know exactly where the venue is and how long it will take to get there. You should also find out the size of the room. If it is large, you may want to discuss the sound system. Find out whether the room is equipped with everything you need for your presentation, such as a slide projector, overhead projector or flip chart.

4. Length of Presentation

Do not be cajoled into speaking for any longer than your information will allow. It is always better to speak for a shorter time rather than over-run. We all have busy schedules, and to waste people's valuable time is a sin.

5. Other Speakers

You need to know if there are any other speakers and, if so, the subject areas they will be addressing so you can avoid repetition.

WRITING THE SPEECH

There are five essential rules when preparing a speech or presentation:

1 You must know your subject.
2 You must be sincere.
3 You should be convinced that your message is worthwhile and that your audience will benefit from it.
4 You must be enthusiastic.
5 You should be self-confident.

One of the things we all fear when we get up to speak is that we will forget everything, including our own name! With careful preparation, however, we will not only remember everything we want to say, but we will also make sure we give our audience all the information it needs in a logical, straightforward and entertaining way. But give yourself time. Preparing any sort of presentation takes hours, not minutes.

When writing a speech, always remember the following point:

Write the talk to be said, not read.

There is an enormous difference between holding someone's attention with the spoken, rather than the written word. When speaking to people, we have to use language that is easily assimilated. If our audience has to try too hard, it will switch off. The English language is one of the richest in the world, but we tend to use only a fraction of the words available to us. Although you should not try to sound as though you have swallowed a dictionary, aim to make your talks as interesting as possible. Whatever your message, make it clear and concise.

The Objective

Start by deciding what you want the talk to achieve. Do you want:

to inform?
to influence?
to recommend a course of action?
to persuade?
to motivate?
to entertain?

When starting to write a speech, talk or presentation, it is a useful exercise to jot down in a sentence the message you want your audience to take away with it. This helps to clarify your thoughts and objective. Here are two examples:

> To convince my colleagues that it would save the company time and money to purchase all our paper from one source.

> To inform the conference that resources spent on training will increase sales and turnover.

Next, put yourself in the audience's shoes. What would *you* want to know if you were listening? If your brief is to talk about a specific problem, take the bull by the horns and mention it straightaway, telling the audience that you are aware of the problem and stating what you are doing to put it right. If people want a particular answer, they will not listen properly until you have satisfied their needs.

Structure and Content

The following guidelines are for talks or presentations of about fifteen minutes in length; anything more than that and you might want an Autocue (for more on such aids, *see page 117*).

Start by writing down everything that could be relevant and of interest. Have a brainstorming session with yourself. Once you have decided what is pertinent, write out a first draft. There are several important reasons for doing this, the first being that you are sure of getting the composition correct. It is easy to think that you know what you want and need to say, but unless the talk is structured properly, both you and the audience can get horribly confused. How many times have you heard speakers repeat themselves simply because they need thinking time, or have lost the direction of the talk?

Opening Remarks and Introduction

It is often said that if you cannot memorize the introduction, it is too long. This is a pretty good rule of thumb. Keep the introduction short, as its purpose is to grab the audience's attention. A quotation or a startling fact is a good way of getting people to listen to you. However you do it, the introduction is the first step down the road of your presentation, and you must make sure the audience stays with you all the way.

Key Points

For the main part of your speech, try to keep to three or four clearly defined points or subjects. Offer your audience something that it needs or wants to know. The greatest incentives for anyone to listen to you are:

> fear
> greed
> topicality
> sex.

In most presentations and speeches, sex usually plays a minor part, unless you are going to tell jokes. Even then it should be used with caution, as you can alienate more people than you amuse! Try to make your information topical and put yourself between the audience and adversity. We are all basically selfish, and unless something has some relevance to us, we are not interested. For instance, if there is news of a motorway accident, the first thought that goes through our mind is 'do I know anyone who was in the area?'. And if we hear of a massive Lottery win, we will read the newspaper the next morning to see if our numbers have come up.

A key point using the incentive of fear might be:

The current system will be obsolete very shortly. It will cost a lot to maintain, and the longer we keep it the more costly it will become. The option I am recommending may seem expensive in the short term; however I believe that to secure the future we have no choice but to replace equipment that is going to put an increasing drain on our resources.

Now using greed:

This new computer system may seem very expensive today, but the savings made in the cost of man hours alone will mean that it will have more than paid for itself by the start of the next financial year.

And topicality:

As you may have seen in the Press last week, the demand for faster, more efficient delivery schedules is increasing rapidly. We at Post-Haste have to be able to meet that demand, so I am recommending a new computer system to be implemented by the end of next month.

Having made a key point, back it up with sufficient detail to prove it, and try to establish a brief but logical link to the next one. The aim is to lift your audience's interest with each point, rather like changing gear in a car. If you can construct your argument to help save your listeners hassle, time or money, you will gain and keep their undivided attention.

Descriptive Phrases

Who said 'a picture paints a thousand words'? Well, it is absolutely true where presentations and speeches are concerned. Any phrases, sayings, anecdotes or analogies that you can use to illustrate a point are worth their weight in gold. Instead of stating that an object weighs 2.2 kilos, try saying it is as heavy as a bag of sugar. When referring to something 20 metres in height, the description 'the height of an average two-storey building' immediately enables listeners to identify with what you are trying to say. This obviously would not apply if you were giving a technical presentation where facts and figures have to be accurate. For non-technical presentations, further examples of descriptive phrases include: 'the initial expenditure will be no more than the price of an average family car' and 'solving the problem was like trying to stop a block of ice melting. Then we suddenly found the fridge'.

Jokes

If you are good at telling jokes, then by all means include some. Do not, however, feel that you have to be a stand-up comic; a joke that falls flat is far worse than no joke at all. Bear in mind the journalists' golden rule: 'if in doubt – leave it out'. This also applies to any information you are unsure about.

The Conclusion

This is a very important part of the talk. Summarize the major points, demonstrating that your objective has been met and make sure the audience knows when you have finished. If a speaker constantly says 'and finally' or 'to summarize', the audience will have switched off long before she has! One useful way of concluding is to link back to the introduction:

> I said at the start of this talk that time is the one thing we have, so let us make the most of it. Thank you.

Do not end with an apology such as 'I don't think there is anything else to say'. Make sure the conclusion finishes on a positive note. For example:

> In conclusion, we have at last found the solution to the problem, and now I suggest we put the recovery plan into action without further delay.

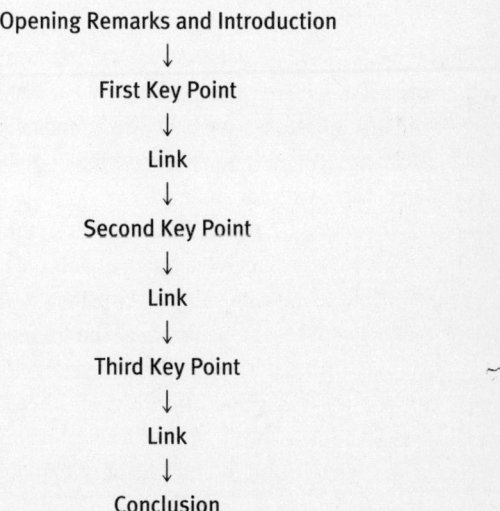

Opening Remarks and Introduction
↓
First Key Point
↓
Link
↓
Second Key Point
↓
Link
↓
Third Key Point
↓
Link
↓
Conclusion

Figure 6.1
A diagram showing the basic structure of a speech.

Checklist

Once you have prepared your talk thoroughly, check these points before you begin rehearsing:

Is your introduction interesting enough to seize the audience's attention?

Are your key points in logical order?

Have you linked each key point with the one before it?

Have you kept everything logical and clear?

Do you need any visual aids? Will they help or distract the audience?

Have you involved your audience by regularly using the words 'we' and 'us'?

Have you been positive throughout?

Will the talk meet its objective?

Is the talk written in a suitably conversational style?

Have you removed any words that jar or are repetitive?

Have you told your audience everything it needs to know (not everything you know!)?

Is the conclusion effective?

REHEARSAL AND PERFORMANCE

I would never advise anyone to learn a presentation word for word, but the better you know it, the more confident you will be. Many people like to put their 'bullet points' on cards, but even if you are planning to read the talk from paper or an Autocue, it is equally important to know it well so that you can keep eye contact with your audience.

One of the best ways to rehearse is to record what you are going to say onto a small tape recorder (not a Dictaphone). It is only by hearing what you plan to say that you can be sure you are not using the same 'pet' words time after time. Make the first recording to check the content, and when you are sure that it is right, record the talk again for delivery. Only by listening can you make certain the message you are trying to convey is clear and to the point. Practise reading the talk in front of a mirror. If you have access to a video camera, so much the better. It is the best learning tool for presentations that I know.

You should always stand when giving anything but a very informal talk. If you are standing, the members of the audience have to look up to you, which gives you a psychological advantage. Even in informal meetings it is a good thing to stand up, as it will help overcome the natural vulnerability that we all feel when we are the focus of attention.

But the focus of attention is what you need to be. In order to get people to listen to you, their whole attention should be focused on you. When you stand up to speak, pause, look round the room and smile! A smile does two important things: it creates a bond with your audience, and relaxes the muscles around the mouth, enabling you to use it properly. Start speaking slightly more slowly than usual, and with your voice at a slightly lower pitch. This is because nerves tend to make us speed up or use the voice's higher register.

If you have a sudden cold or sore throat when you are about to make an important presentation, try 'Vocal Zones' lozenges, which are used by many actors and singers (including Cliff Richard) to aid the voice. They are available at smaller pharmacies and health food shops.

It is not always what we say, but the way in which we say it that makes people retain the message. There are three important elements to bring to any presentation – the three 'e's: energy, enthusiasm and enjoyment.

1   **Energy** comes from knowing what you need to say and wanting to say it.
2   **Enthusiasm** – If you are not enthusiastic about your subject, then why should anyone else be?
3   **Enjoyment** comes from having prepared thoroughly, so that you look forward to imparting the information.

Body Language

Once more, body language is important. Swaying, coughing, wringing the hands or any other diverting mannerisms act as a distraction. Stand with one foot slightly in front of the other as this helps you to keep reasonably still. However confident your voice may sound, if you are weaving like a snake in front of your audience you will appear neither confident nor competent. Remember, you are the expert when the spotlight is on you, and your audience needs to be able to trust in your ability to deliver whatever it is that you are trying to sell them. Whether this is a product, a service, an idea or yourself, you have got to put the message over in an interesting, informative and dynamic fashion.

Mannerisms to guard against include:

shifting from foot to foot
rubbing the nose or eyes
wandering around
wringing the hands
fiddling with jewellery
stroking the cheeks or chin
playing with hair.

All these characteristics are tell-tale signs that you are not as confident as you would like to be, so try to avoid them. Eye contact is essential if you are to know how your audience is reacting, so try to look at each member of the audience at some time during your presentation. The old directive that suggested a speaker looked at a spot just over people's heads has been updated, thank goodness! You should be able to control your audience like a conductor governs an orchestra, building them up and letting them down to keep their interest and attention.

There are eight pertinent points that help the delivery of a speech:

1   Pace – variations of speed.
2   Pitch – not too high or low. Feel comfortable.
3   Phrasing – think about what you are saying. Emphasize stress points.
4   Projection – not shouting. Produce your voice with plenty of controlled breathing.
5   Pause – very important. It gives your audience a chance to absorb what you are saying.
6   Posture – relaxed and upright. It is not only important for good appearance, but is also essential for correct breathing.
7   Preparation – fundamental.
8   Practice – it really does make perfect!

Delivery Self-check

Use the following checklist when practising your delivery:

Was my purpose fulfilled? Did I impress, inform, convince?
Was my message clear?

Was my subject well rehearsed?

Did I complement the other speakers?

Was my voice enthusiastic?

Did I come across sincerely?

Were my pauses used to good effect?

Did my face show my feelings?

Were my introduction and conclusion effective?

Did I look natural?

Was the rhythm of my speech good or was it inconsistent or monotonous?

Did I speak too slowly or too quickly?

Taking Questions

When you answer questions, usually at the end of your talk, your presentation is not over – you are still 'under the spotlight'. A positive ending to a talk might go like this:

> I have given you all the information we have to date, so are there any questions?

This is a time when you can expand on some points, but do not let yourself be dragged into a debate with one particularly verbose or disgruntled individual. If you are addressing a large gathering, it is a good idea to repeat the question so that the rest of the audience is sure what has been asked. As you start to answer, look at the person who has voiced the question, and then start to take in the rest of the room. If someone is very persistent and will not let a subject go, you could reply thus:

> As we have not got too much time I would like to move on, but let's meet afterwards so that we can get to grips with your specific problem.

REPEATING THE TALK

Once you have given a talk, you will probably use it again many times, but adapted for different audiences. It is most important to revamp your talk for each audience. You will get a much better response and it does not take long.

When adapting a talk, it can help to work through the following points:

What part will your talk play in the event, meeting or conference?

Are there any other speakers?

Has the objective changed? If so, write out a complete sentence which
describes it.

Think carefully about the people who will comprise your audience.

Write down what your audience will need to know and want to hear.

Check that your introduction is still appropriate and change any key
points to suit this group.

If possible, introduce a local aspect or something particularly relevant to
the audience.

VISUAL AIDS

The visual aid is there to help the audience comprehend the message, and
it should not be used as a prompt for the speaker. How many times have
you seen people talking to the screen, sometimes completely turning their
back on the group they are addressing? Having said that, speakers (and
their audiences) find that slides enliven a presentation. Graphs, charts and
diagrams can be used to explain complex ideas and information. Text slides
emphasize the structure of a talk and lead the audience through the points
the speaker wishes to cover. Illustrations used during a speech tell a story
without the speaker having to give complicated information, thus reinforcing
ideas and helping audience involvement.

The Secret of Good Slides

There is really only one secret to good slides and that is simplicity. Each
slide should be used to make one point only. Slides which contain too much
information or illustration look cluttered and are difficult to follow. Too many
words make the text small and difficult to read. As a general guideline it is
best to have only six lines of text per slide and six words per line. Graphs and
diagrams should be similarly uncluttered. If you feel that it is really important
for your audience to have information in the form of complicated tables or
diagrams, it is better to give them a hard copy in their conference papers.

For an average presentation of forty to forty-five minutes it is most
effective to show approximately one slide every two minutes. This does not

mean, however, that you have to use twenty slides, but more than this number would probably be too many for your audience.

To prepare for using visual aids in your presentation, ask yourself the following questions (the same principles apply to using flip charts, overhead projector [OHP] transparencies and 35-millimetre slides):

What facilities are available at the venue?

How big/dark/light is the room?

How much time and money is available?

At which points of the presentation will visual aids be used?

Will they be used again? (If so, store them carefully in a box or envelope.)

Do you have to carry the equipment or visual aids off-site?

What is the message you want your slides to convey?

Is it best conveyed in words or pictures?

If the information is very technical, would a handout be better?

Guidelines

OHP transparencies should be computer generated wherever possible.

Use no more words per slide than you can write on a T-shirt.

Do not display tables of figures – convert them instead into graphs, pie charts or histograms.

Use colours – choose contrasting ones and not too many.

Use big, bold letters, whether they are handwritten or typed (5 millimetres for flip charts, 1–2 millimetres for OHP transparencies). Do not use fine OHP pens.

Leave a border around the transparency – do not write up to the edge.

Mounting the transparency will help ensure it is straight on the OHP. You can also use the mounts to make useful notes.

Use symbols instead of words sometimes.

Cartoons carry a lot of impact as the audience is more likely to remember something humorous.

Select information – highlight key words in bold.

See how the transparency looks when projected and make any necessary changes.

By laying one transparency over the other (overlays) you can gradually build up information. Overlays should always be well mounted.

Masking allows you to reveal one idea at a time so the audience is not distracted. It is much safer to attach masks to the mount rather than using a sheet of paper which invariably slides off.

Give all your slides a final check on the OHP before the presentation.

Using Visual Aids

Make sure that all members of the audience can see the display. It takes some practice to use a flip chart or an overhead projector properly.

Overhead Projector (OHP)

A pointer is a useful device when using the OHP. Point on the glass rather than at the screen if possible, as this will stop you being tempted to turn your back on the audience. Stand to one side and keep your eyes on the people you are talking to, checking from time to time that the acetates are straight. Continue talking when you change them so that you do not break the flow of the presentation.

Flip Chart

When writing on a flip chart, wait until you have finished and turned to face the group before continuing.

Slide Projector

It is advisable to become familiar with a slide projector before using it, and to rehearse if someone else is going to change the slides for you. As before, stand to one side and talk to your audience. The screen is not interested in anything you have to say!

Handouts

Any information that needs time to be assimilated should be given out in written form after the presentation. If it is waiting on the seats, your audience will be reading it rather than listening to you. The only exception is at large conferences where the speech is printed so that the audience can follow while it is being read. Personally, I do not see the point of this. There is no incentive for the speaker to 'entertain' an audience if it is reading every word, and this gives rise to boring presentations. If the text is available as a handout afterwards, it allows ample opportunity to go over any points that might have been missed.

Autocue

The Autocue is a marvellous invention! Teleprompter, the version used in television studios, has transformed newsreading and presenting, and it is now being used widely on the conference circuit. It consists of a small glass screen attached to a lectern which displays the text to the reader but not the audience. The operator needs to see the script beforehand in order to type it into the machine, unless you provide a disk. Then he or she should run it according to your reading speed.

It is essential not to ad-lib! My boss at the BBC used to say that the only good ad-lib was a rehearsed ad-lib, and it is certainly true in this case. If you digress from the script, the Autocue operator will have no idea where you are, and this can lead to all sorts of trouble.

CHECKLIST

Photocopy this checklist and work through it while at the planning stages of every presentation you do:

number of people in audience	☐
ages of audience	☐
sex of audience	☐
job categories/levels of audience	☐
reason for attending	☐
audience attitude	☐
handouts	☐
seating arrangements	☐
visual aids	☐
microphones	☐
starting and finishing times	☐
catering arrangements	☐

7

vive la difference!

Over the last fifty years, differences in the way in which men and women work, dress and behave have been diminishing. Although women have always done men's jobs, they have never before had the equality enjoyed today. With equal opportunities, pay and conditions in many industries, the prospects for working women, on the whole, have never been brighter.

In some ways, however, a woman's life has never been harder. Women are now suffering more stress than their mothers generally did, and are more prone to 'businessman's ailments' such as heart disease and ulcers. Women make up a crucial part of the workforce; but we are different to men, and should capitalize on those differences. Women listen better; they are generally more understanding, trying to see all points of view; and they tend to put more consideration into decision making.

WORKING WOMEN

With more women choosing to work, as well as those who work through economic necessity, female influence in the workplace is growing. Up until now, women have had to perform very much like men – only better – to achieve management positions. While this is still sometimes the case, the natural female style of more supportive administration is proving successful as well as popular.

ASSERTIVENESS

There is a big difference between being aggressive and being assertive. Assertiveness helps us become more confident about ourselves and in our relationships with others, both socially and in the workplace. Being assertive is about focusing on the specific results we wish to achieve while maintaining flexibility in the way we achieve them.

Assertiveness means standing up for your opinions and beliefs without denigrating those of others. Everyone has a right to an opinion, and it is important to state yours clearly and explain why you hold it. You will sound more confident if your convictions are based on rational, researched arguments rather than emotions or feelings.

Women are inclined to say things like 'Well, I think we could...' or 'Maybe we should consider...', sounding as if they are not too sure about their recommendations. If you sound unsure, nobody will believe you and you will lose credibility. Using phrases such as the following will help:

- 'This is how I see the situation...'
- 'This is what I believe and why...'
- 'This is what I want and why...'
- 'In my opinion we should do x, y and z, and if we do, the outcome will be...'

In group exercises at work, women will still often take a supportive role. They may take notes so that they do not play an active part in the decision-making process and are not, therefore, in a prime position for an appraisal. Be assertive. If you do not want a subordinate role, do not play it! Much of the problem stems from childhood. Girls tend to play in small groups, or with one particular friend, whereas boys play in larger groups. Boys' games are very much concerned with status, and they tend to find natural leaders who organize the rest of the gang. Girls who show the same tendencies are accused of being bossy, and are taught to stand back and let others take a turn.

Often, men and women have very different ways of saying what they mean. Sometimes it can almost be a mutually unintelligible language! Lessons learned in childhood continue in the workplace, and this can often put women at a disadvantage. A man will automatically take the credit for work he (and sometimes his department) has done, but many women use the word 'we' when referring to tasks that they have completed alone. They somehow imagine that their boss or the rest of the department will realize that the credit should go to them alone, but this rarely happens.

Women tend to apologize more than men, but when they say 'I'm sorry' it is often meant as a way of expressing concern rather than a statement of apology. People who are constantly apologizing may end up appearing weaker and less confident than they actually are. Men apologize far less on the whole as they hate to admit fault unless they really have to.

You have to be assertive when dealing with men. Unless you tell them straight, they do not read between the lines. Take the scenario of having to tell a salesman that late appointments are starting to lose business for the firm. A typical female approach is to consider the good sales record and then come to the problem of being 'rather late on a few occasions'. He seems to take the message on board, but there are continuing complaints. When she tackles him again, he is surprised and says that he thought she said he was doing fine. When tackling any criticism it is vital to be tactful and polite, but the message must get through. The conversation might go something like this:

Jim, I have been wanting to talk to you about Walker Bros. It seem you have been late for the last three appointments, and they are not very happy. It would be a pity to spoil such a good sales record, wouldn't it? So I'm sure it won't happen again.

Said with a smile, this takes the sting out of the tale without losing authority.

Women pay others more compliments than men do, so if you ask a male colleague what he thought of your performance in a meeting, do not be surprised if you get an honest answer, rather than the 'Oh, fine' or 'really good' you might receive from another woman. Men are more likely to socialize with their superiors at work, eating with them at lunchtime, for example, to get themselves noticed. Women, on the other hand, are often afraid of sending out the wrong signals or appearing pushy.

Women still fail to grasp opportunities as well as men do. For example, they are not as good at networking with their own sex. They are much more reticent about ringing somebody up to ask them out to lunch, even though there may be important business to discuss. This is because many women, especially younger ones, think they may be projecting the wrong image by being assertive. Making contacts is an important part of success in any business, so do not be afraid to arrange a lunch date, either to talk business or just to get to know someone better.

Women also have different ways of talking about their achievements. Again, the reason for this goes back to childhood. Boys tend to maximize their achievements in order to be looked up to by their peers, whereas girls play theirs down.

Although I would hate the idea that men and women should start behaving in the same way, it is useful to know how the other half thinks, and use the information to our advantage when we have to.

AGGRESSION

An aggressive woman will not make a good manager, especially if the workforce is predominantly male. If you tell, rather than ask, people to do something and rule the roost with a heavy hand, life will not be easy for anyone.

The iron fist in the velvet glove is a better approach. It is important not be a pushover, but listening is a great skill, and one of the most significant in people management. Examples of an aggressive stance might be:

'Get this into the post by five o'clock.'
'Don't argue! The reason we are going to proceed this way, is because it is the best way.'
'There will be a departmental meeting this afternoon – be there!'

Rather than:

'Please make sure this gets into the post by five o'clock.'
'I can see you have a very good point, but the reason we are going to proceed this way is because it is the best strategy for the whole department.'
'There will be a meeting at two o'clock. It is important, so I look forward to seeing you all there.'

These examples may seem painfully obvious, but can you honestly say you have never spoken aggressively under duress? I know I can't.

CHILDREN

As salaries increase so do responsibilities. These days companies expect 100 per cent from senior executives, and because they are generally paying women the same as men, they expect the same commitment. That is fine for women who have no children, but it does not leave much time for family life. It is a problem that has not really been solved satisfactorily. Although it is possible to have a career and a family, there has to be compromise.

It seems unfair that, while it is acceptable for men to talk about their children at work and be seen to take an active interest in their welfare, women hardly dare mention them, and would rather say they are leaving early to go to the dentist than admit there is a sick child at home. We wanted equality and we have got it. The problem is that we have to carry the babies and should nurture them, if possible, for the first few weeks of life. Some large organizations have good maternity schemes which keep jobs open for up to two years after the baby is born, giving the mother a chance to decide whether or not she wants to return to work. Many companies, however, now recruit on a fixed-term contract basis. This means they do not have to pay maternity benefit and will certainly not keep jobs open. When applying for jobs, find out your maternity entitlements from the human resources manager.

Some jobs demand very long hours and real dedication to reach top, or even upper-management, positions. In many cases, women have to work even harder than their male counterparts. Try to create a balance between the office and leisure pursuits. Meeting people from outside your sphere of work once or twice a month could make a positive difference. Being personally fulfilled is part of being a good manager, as personal frustrations are damaging if allowed to spill over into professional life.

Should working women bother to have children if they are going to be away from them all day? Many working mothers are asked this question. The answer is yes, of course they should, but with certain provisos. Children blame their parents if they feel they are getting a bad deal. This can be very hurtful and upsetting, sometimes making it difficult to present the right image at work.

If your child screams blue murder until the minute you have driven out of sight and then stops, you do not have much of a problem. If, however, your child cries for a long time, or is withdrawn and solitary at home or at school, then you have to ask yourself which is more important – the career or the child. Certainly, trying to do the washing, ironing, shopping and cooking as well as creating a positive image at work is not easy. Supporting the children in their various activities both during and after school also takes some juggling.

If your partner is supportive, this will help enormously. To be able to share the role of bringing up the children works to everyone's best advantage. It is important to lay the ground rules early on, as it is more difficult to expect your man to find the ballet clothes or make packed lunches if he is blissfully unaware of the extra time and organization needed. Try to determine which chores and activities suit your respective work patterns and make a list of who does what.

If you have the sort of job that leaves you overtired, stressed out and unable to take your mind off problems back at the office, then you will not succeed either domestically or professionally. You have to ask yourself whether that would be fair on you or the children. It is also essential for working mothers to have the best possible childcare arrangements in place when they return to work. It is impossible to function happily and efficiently if you are worried about what may be happening at home.

After being awake for most of the night looking after a small child, it is tempting to rush into the office, skirt creased and hair unwashed. Unfortunately, depending on the job, there are many others ready to take your place if standards start to slip. To create the required image in today's competitive world, you need all the help you can get, so I have included some information on the best way to find the support that suits you best.

CHILDCARE

Finding appropriate help can be a problem. When you employ someone, it essential to define the job, responsibilities and the degree of discipline expected right at the start, then everybody knows where they stand.

Au Pairs

Au pairs are young people, usually female, from abroad who are employed in the home to help with childcare. They tend to live with you as part of the family, and only expect to do a limited amount of housework. They need time to go to college, as they are primarily in this country to learn English. Salaries vary, but £30 a week with free food and accommodation is currently around the norm. Check with friends or an agency to get an idea of suitable hours.

You can employ au pairs through an agency (they are listed in *The Lady* magazine, local papers and telephone directories), or you might find one through friends or business contacts. When selecting an au pair, it is important to make sure that she speaks at least some English. When you are about to dash out to work, it is very wearing to be met with a blank stare after you have slowly and carefully given instructions about the children's tea for the tenth time. It is essential to take up references, and not just from an agency. Try and speak to families for whom the au pair has worked in the past.

If it is the au pair's first job, and your work means you are going to be out all day, choose somebody who is not too young and has younger brothers or sisters, so that she has some experience of coping with children. Children can be very cruel, and as soon as they realize a girl cannot understand what they are saying or is too shy to exert any influence over them, they will run rings round her! You should also ensure that the au pair gets used to being in the car with you before expecting her to drive the children, especially if she has never driven on the left before.

Mother's Helps

Many of the guidelines given above for hiring an au pair also apply when taking on a mother's help. Although a mother's help may be as experienced as a qualified nanny, she will not necessarily have any qualifications and may be quite young. Like the au pair, the mother's help's main role is to look after the children, although she will also help with the housework. Unlike the au pair, mother's helps tend to live locally and to arrive at your home daily rather than live in. Again, wages, hours and duties should be ascertained from agencies and sorted out at the interview stage, and you can expect to pay around £140 to £160 a week.

Nannies

Nannies are qualified professionals trained in childcare. They may have graduated from training schools such as Princess Christian or Norland Nannies. The recognized qualification is the NNEB (National Nursery Education Board) certificate.

A nanny's job is specifically to look after the children, but that includes doing their laundry, keeping bedrooms and playroom clean and tidy and cooking and supervising the children's meals. Live-in nannies will expect a pleasant bedroom equipped with a television and perhaps a hi-fi, and probably the use of a car. A good nanny is worth her weight in gold because you know that she is thoroughly responsible and will bring up the children to a high standard. Good nannies do not come cheap, however. The average weekly wage in London is around £150 to £250 a week plus board and lodgings. Some nannies 'job share' these days, working for more than one family, so it is worth asking around. It is advisable to have accident insurance to cover your nanny or indeed anyone who works with you but she is responsible for insuring her belongings. Contact your local authority for the latest advice.

Day Nurseries, Childminders and Crèches

Day nurseries are run both by local councils and, increasingly, by the private sector. If your working hours tend to be standard, a nursery can be a good childcare option, but if you have to work late regularly, you may have problems collecting your child at the end of the day. Try and find a nursery that is most conveniently located for you.

Crèches work on the same principle as day nurseries but tend to accept younger children. If you are lucky, your company may run its own subsidized crèche. Childminders are usually self-employed mothers who will look after children (including their own). They have to be registered by the local authority, which requires a police check of their home. Childminders will take babies as young as a few weeks old, and so will some crèches, but the average age of children starting childcare is around eighteen months to two years. Some establishments educate the children gently; others just encourage them to play. Prices vary from area to area.

When choosing childcare, the most important factor is your child's happiness. You can tell whether children are happy with your choice by what they say about it, and the friends they make. Local papers and directories will give names and numbers of childcare facilities, but do go and see them a number of times before making your decision. The best recommendations come from children themselves, if they are old enough, and from their parents if they are not.

Whichever option you choose, try and give yourself enough time to get ready in the mornings so that you all have a good start to the day. At night, put out your child's clothes and your own.

MEN ABOUT THE HOUSE

As women are no longer dependent on men, it is not surprising that we are marrying later, if at all, and having children later too. The roles for some men and women have completely reversed, with the husband or partner staying at home to look after children while the wife goes out to work. Certainly, most young women today expect their partner to share household tasks and take an active role in bringing up any children.

It is more difficult for older women to come to terms with this shift in emphasis. Those who have been brought up to look after a husband and family as part of their duty find it almost impossible to delegate the chores, and often end up doing everything themselves, even if the husband has retired or is not working. As we go into the next century, our expectations are very different. These days, women's expectations are very high. We are told that we are high achievers, and in many cases we have had to work harder than our male counterparts to reach the same positions. I believe, however, that we must never lose our respect for the opposite sex, otherwise the fair and harmonious relationships we desire will never come about.

The writer and broadcaster Penny Junor and her husband James Leith have four children, ranging from seven to twenty-one. When Penny was asked to write the biography of Prime Minister John Major, the book had to be completed very quickly, so James offered to look after the children, leaving her free to write. That was in 1992, but the arrangement has continued. In fact, it has worked so well that James has written a book, *Ironing John*, about his experiences (*see Bibliography*).

James believes he has a positive mental attitude to whatever he does, and thinks that having been an actor, a restaurateur and a business consultant means that he has never actually seen himself as fitting into a particular slot. 'The problem with some men who have spent the last twenty-five years climbing the corporate ladder, is that they think of themselves in terms of what they do, rather than who they are. I have never had that sort of CV, so I think of myself in terms of the family rather than a specific career or job.' For this type of fundamental role reversal to work, the relationship must be sound and the people involved secure in themselves.

Money can be a thorny issue. A working woman who is earning more than her partner should be careful not to cut the ground from under his feet. The recent changes in the workplace have happened so quickly that men have not had time to come to terms with the fact that they may no longer be the main breadwinner in the family. If a woman makes a big thing of doling out money to a husband at home, she will be undermining him unnecessarily which will be counterproductive for the whole family. It is just as important for a woman at home to be given the same respect; but as a gender we have had to fight for our liberation from being seen as 'goods and chattels' and we are more able to cope.

Redundancy is a traumatic experience for anybody, but worse for the male, who has been accustomed to providing for his family. Losing status often means losing self-respect, so men need to feel that they still have a worthwhile role to play. The piece of mind brought by knowing that the children are being looked after by their father rather than a nanny, no matter how marvellous, is tremendous. Most working mothers really need a good wife – failing that, a good husband!

A working mother who comes home every night when the children are asleep knows she is making a sacrifice. This sort of existence, however, is going to become the norm for more and more mothers who work. In these days of equality, couples will decide who is going to progress faster up the career path and therefore earn more, and that partner will be the breadwinner. If that is the case, couples have to make allowances for each other, and ensure they both have time to enjoy the children as well as benefiting materially.

For men left at home, life can be quite lonely. Women chatting at the school gates about fashions and facials do not want them butting in, and men cannot really join 'ladies' lunches' which help pass the time between housework and school-runs for many mothers. Fulfilling the conventional woman's role can leave some men feeling like part of an alien race. If your husband or partner is running the household, it is important to encourage him to have an outside interest, as well as trying to include him as much as possible in any decision making.

WOMEN AT HOME

If you do not have a career these days, it is easy to feel insignificant. As most people realize, however, bringing up a family is one of the most important jobs you could have, and that is how you should look at it. The positive image that you project will mean you are taken seriously. If you are lucky enough to be able to stay at home, and do not wish to work, then why not make the most of it? It is important, though, not to lose touch with what is going on in the world.

Many women reach the age of forty and look into the mirror thinking 'what have I done with my life?' This is a sad state of affairs, as they may have brought up a family or supported a partner. But what have they done for themselves? Many marriages break up after twenty or more years because the only thing that has kept the couple together has been the children, and when they have flown the nest there is nothing left.

Improving Your Knowledge Base

I have always found it important to keep up with your partner and children. This is easier if you are working because there is outside stimulus, but there is plenty you can do if you are at home. When children reach their teens they tend to think they know all there is to know about life, and anyone over the age of twenty-five has had it! There are various courses on offer at colleges all around the country. You might enjoy learning another language, improving your culinary skills, painting, pottery, even sitting GCSEs or 'A' levels. The people you meet are usually very interesting, and to have a lively discussion about Descartes over the dinner table with your progeny can be very stimulating! If the idea of attending classes does not appeal to you, The Open University runs correspondence courses in a wide range of subjects, as do numerous other organizations.

Even if you only read the newspaper every day (preferably one of the broadsheets) you will keep yourself abreast of current affairs. Reading the financial pages will enable you to join in discussions regarding business matters. This will also stand you in very good stead should you decide to go back to work.

Returning to Work

Running a house is excellent training for the workplace, and provides experience that can be of enormous benefit to women returning to work. Large organizations, such as Microsoft, are increasingly looking for the sort of transferable skills that women at home perform every day. Doing the laundry, polishing the furniture, arranging dental appointments and preparing the dinner (to name but a few of the myriad household chores that we do automatically every day) enables us to become experts in time management, flexible working hours and organizational skills.

LOOKING GOOD ON A BUDGET

Children are expensive. As a mother, whether at home or at work, you may find that creating a positive image for you and your children requires careful financial planning. These days there is no stigma attached to buying nearly new clothes. There are now specialist shops and boutiques in most towns that cater for this expanding market. Indeed, for children, it is sensible to buy second-hand clothes, as they often outgrow their clothes before wearing them out. You can pick up some marvellous bargains. I have bought designer jackets and suits that do not look as though they have ever been off the hanger, at a fraction of the price I would have expected to pay in the shops. If you combine a career with motherhood, something has to give, so you have to be prepared to make some compromises.

ANTI-STRESS BREAKS

For women wanting to create a positive image, it is a good idea to take a break that will really recharge the batteries.

Health Farms
Health farms used to be the domain of overstressed, overweight males. Now, women from all walks of life are finding that the massages and other treatments on offer are a real boost in a busy schedule. They are priced from around £90 a night, and most have special offers. I have listed details of a few below.

Champneys Health Resort
Wiggington, Tring, Hertfordshire
This is one of the most famous health farms. For a minimum two-night stay, it will cost between £300 and £1,000, depending on the room.

Forest Mere Health Hydro
Liphook, Hampshire
This is ideal for those who prefer quality rather than quantity, and a more serious attitude to health. Prices from around £250 to £450 for a minimum three-night stay.

Hoar Cross Hall Health Spa
Yoxall, Staffordshire
Used by quite a number of women-only groups, it also operates as a corporate conference centre. Minimum two-night stay starts from £200.

Ragdale Hall Health Hydro
Melton Mowbray, Leicestershire
Caters especially for women and has an impressive range of beauty treatments. Prices from £168.

Shrubland Hall Health Clinic
Coddenham, Suffolk
The accent is very much on health, fitness and diet, and the clientele is slightly older than average. A three-night stay costs from around £390.

Stobo Castle Health Spa
Peeblesshire, Scotland
There is a lovely, friendly atmosphere in this beautiful Scottish castle. It has under fifty guests and is known for its generous treatment package and marvellous food! A two-night stay costs from around £280.

Beauty Days
If you have neither the time nor the money for a break in a health farm, treating yourself to a beauty day is a good option. These are often run by large department stores and give you lots of tips to help improve diet and fitness, as well as guidance on skin care and make-up. Listed below are just a few of the salons around, and there are more open in the provinces now. A spot of pampering does a huge amount to boost the ego as well as the batteries, so do not think of it as a luxury, but as an investment in your most powerful weapon – you.

Harrods Hair and Beauty Clinic
5th Floor, Harrods, Knightsbridge, London
Their 'Ultimate Day of Beauty' will set you back about £300, but includes eight hours of top-to-toe beauty treatments.

The Sanctuary
12 Floral street, Covent Garden, London
This is a women-only salon open seven days a week. Membership is around £40 per day for the use of pool, sauna, steam room and sunbeds. Treatments are charged separately.

The Spa, Selfridges
400 Oxford Street, London W1
Their 'Relaxation Day' is priced around £55 and includes sea salt glow, steam room, sauna and massage.

Elizabeth Arden Red Door Salon at Simpson
34 Jermyn Street, London
If you are going out for the evening, they offer a 'Pre-Theatre Dash' for about £30. Their 'Main Chance Day' costs around £140, which includes massage, make-up, hair-do and a light lunch.

8

---

manners maketh woman

'Misunderstandings do not exist, only the failure to communicate exists' (Southeast Asian proverb). Misunderstandings can often be misinterpreted as bad manners, so it is important to get the communication right. But what are manners today, and do they matter?

Good manners are an essential part of a positive image. Before attending a business or social engagement, preparation is vital. Find out as much as you can about the place you are going to, the people who will be there and what is expected of you. It is a good idea to read relevant books and magazines about business and social etiquette. If in doubt, never be afraid to ask for advice. Most people take it as a compliment, and unless you feel you are going to lose face, it is usually the quickest way to get reliable, up-to-date information.

MANNERS

Manners and etiquette are not quite the same thing. In her book *Modern Etiquette*, Moyra Bremner aptly defines the difference thus: 'Etiquette concerns the letter of the law, whereas manners are governed by its spirit.' People with good manners treat others with civility, think of others before themselves and have respect for each other. These days, some women take exception when men offer them a seat or open a door for them as they see it as patronizing. In my view, this is a shame, as it deters men from doing it for women who may consider it an act of common courtesy.

Having good manners means behaving in a way that is socially acceptable, in business as well as domestic life. If we all followed the guidelines of good manners and mutual respect, we would treat each other more kindly, behave more honestly and enjoy both professional and social success.

ETIQUETTE

Standard etiquette usually reflects the manners and behaviour of a society's most successful group, which in Europe means the aristocracy and the professional classes. Etiquette has provided us with codes for behaving in a civilized fashion. Unfortunately, it has also supplied us with trivial rules that can be divisive, revealing which stratum of society we come from. Many of the more obscure codes of social behaviour are now obsolete, but there are some guidelines that still prevail. Whether or not you want to adhere to the rules, it is as well to know what the establishment regards as 'right'. To know how to behave in any society gives you enormous confidence, but it is important not to get so bogged down with the rights and wrongs that we cease to be ourselves or fail to enjoy a social evening.

Codes of etiquette change over the years, and what is acceptable today was probably 'not quite the thing' a few years ago. Putting on make-up in public, for example, was never done. It is still not a good idea, but you can get away with it in some situations, such as when travelling on trains or planes when you would risk breaking your neck attempting to apply it in the privacy of the loo! The fact that more women use swear words these days does not make swearing any more congenial. Keep your language as clean as possible, otherwise it will catch you out when you least expect it. Mine used to be rather colourful at times. I once uttered a rather choice word on live television after making a rather silly mistake – not something I ever wish to repeat. Coarse talk is just as bad as swearing, as it can create a very negative impression.

TABLE MANNERS

Being confronted by a glittering array of knives and forks can be quite daunting. It is all very well to heed the advice 'wait to see which one everybody else uses before you start', but what if you are the guest of honour and everybody is waiting for you? It is not easy to present a confident image if you use the fruit knife instead of the fish knife, or use a fork to eat asparagus when served on its own.

In my view, good table manners are essential. I am appalled by some of the very senior people I meet who can hardly hold a knife and fork, and eat in such a cumbersome way that it becomes distracting. If you spend a business lunch concentrating on whether your companion's food is actually going to make the mouth, rather than on what the person is saying, the whole episode can be counterproductive. Contracts have been won and lost on the tilt of a knife or the slurping of soup.

Our upbringing strongly influences our table manners. If children never sit down to a family meal, it not only deprives them of the chance to join in discussions involving the whole family, but it also denies them the opportunity to learn good table manners.

Handling Cutlery Correctly

Here are some guidelines for handling cutlery:

- Tuck the handle of a knife into the heel of the right hand (if you are right-handed), with the index finger on top of it, pointing towards the blade. Do not hold the knife like a pen.
- Hold the fork in a similar fashion, prongs towards the plate.
- The soup and pudding spoons are held like a pen, but across the body and parallel to the table.
- When used alone, the prongs of the fork face upwards, unless you are cutting food.
- When you are not eating, put the utensils on the plate in a slight V shape, (to show that you have not finished). The handles should never rest on the table.
- In Europe it is correct to use the knife and fork together, whereas in America the food is cut up with both implements, then the fork is put in the right hand to eat.

- Keep your elbows close to your sides and hands low.
- Lift food up to the mouth, rather than dipping the head to meet it.
- It is not 'correct' to put a fork under the plate to enable the sauce to gather at one end.

Which Implement to Use When

The table is usually laid so that every implement, except the soup spoon and the bread or butter knife, has a partner, but you do not always use both. When confronted by a frightening array of silver, a good rule of thumb is to start at the outside and work your way in. This rule is not foolproof, however, as some people lay the bread or small knife on the side plate, some put it above the plate under the pudding spoon and fork and others place it to the left or right of the big knives. Do not be daunted if you make a mistake – either carry on eating with confidence (most people will not notice anyway) or acknowledge the fact that you always get confused and start again.

The classic way to set the table is thus:

On the Right

- Soup spoon on the outside.
- Next to it, the bread knife.
- Then the knife for the main course.
- Next to it, the pudding spoon.

On the Left

- The main-course fork on the outside.
- The pudding fork next to it.

Obviously, if you have more courses you will need more cutlery. Serrated knives are used only in restaurants, even for steak; but fish knives, which had been out of fashion for some time, are enjoying a comeback, except for oysters.

Tackling Tricky Food

With more and more foreign food now being eaten in this country, there are even more dishes to choose from and more decisions to be made on how to eat them. Here are some guidelines.

- Rice and pasta should be eaten with a fork held in the right hand, prongs facing upwards.
- Pâté is eaten only with a knife.
- Puddings (sweets) should be eaten with both spoon and fork. A teaspoon should be used for puddings served in a glass or small bowl.
- Asparagus is finger food and should only be eaten with a knife and fork when mixed with other vegetables. On its own, it should be held at the fat end, and the tips dipped into the sauce which has been poured onto the plate.
- Globe artichokes are also finger food. If the middle leaves have been removed, the sauce goes in the hole, otherwise it goes on the plate. Pull off the outer leaves and dip the fleshy end into the sauce, biting hard enough to remove the flesh as you pull the leaf out of your mouth. Put discarded leaves on the plate provided, and when you reach the succulent base, eat it with a knife and fork.
- Frog's legs are eaten with the fingers, as are spare ribs.
- Game used to be the only meat that was eaten in the fingers, but now one uses a knife and fork for the sinewy legs, unless your host suggests otherwise.
- Oysters and mussels should be lifted out of the shell with a fork (the French use a discarded mussel shell as a pair of pincers). Only the juice of an oyster should be drunk from a shell, otherwise use a soup spoon to finish any liquid. The empty shells should be put on the plate provided.
- Snails are held by the shells with special tongs, and the snail twisted out with a sharp fork.
- If prawns and shrimps are served in their shells, take off the head with your fingers and lift the shell away from the body before removing the tail. Once shelled, they are eaten with a knife and fork. Finger bowls as well as napkins should be provided. Incidentally, finger bowls should be filled with cold water, as this does not open the pores and allow odours to penetrate the skin.
- A savoury soufflé is always eaten with a fork, whereas a sweet one is eaten with a spoon.
- The correct way to consume soup is to push the spoon away from you as you scoop it up, and then sip it from the side of the spoon. In this country it is not done to lift or tip the bowl, unlike in Japan, where the bowl is lifted to the mouth.

- Corn on the cob is rolled in butter and then bitten into carefully while holding it at each end with the fingers or special holders. Leaning your elbows on the table makes eating this rather unwieldy vegetable even less elegant!

- Crab and lobster are rather a fiddle to eat unless the flesh has been dressed and put back into the shells. Larger claws have to be broken with a cracker and then the meat is scooped out with a lobster pick. For the smaller claws, use the fingers then eat the meat with a knife and fork. Brown bread and butter is served to be eaten with crab, not to have the meat spread on it. Both these shellfish can be rather messy to eat, so finger bowls and good-sized napkins are advisable.

- Eat fish off the bone rather than fillet it on the plate. Remove the fine bones with your knife and fork and put them on one side. If you get one in your mouth, discreetly make a fist with your hand and deposit the bone into it before putting it on your plate.

- Fruit can be a problem too. Oranges have been known to drench the person sitting next to you, and ripe mangoes will probably do the same to you. On more formal occasions, fruit is halved with a knife and then eaten either with a knife and fork or with the fingers.

- Cherry stones and grape pips are best dealt with in the same way as fish bones. Grapes should be cut or pulled off in small clusters. Melons and paw-paws are eaten with a spoon or a knife and fork, and kiwis should be cut in half and then eaten with a teaspoon.

- In Britain it is correct to break bread rolls rather than cut them. When buttering, put the butter onto your plate first, and then apply to a small piece of bread at a time, rather than the whole piece. It is also polite to spread pâté, cheese or jams the same way.

- Canapés and dips are very popular at drinks parties. When encouraged to 'have a little more', one is left in a quandary as to whether to remember the rules of basic hygiene or go ahead and dunk again. As Moyra Bremner says, 'follow the one dip per chip rule' or at least turn the crisp or piece of crudité round and use the unlicked end. Put used sausage sticks or olive stones onto an empty plate or, if there is nowhere else available, into your pocket (or your partner's)!

- Salt should be poured onto the edge of the plate or taken with a spoon (even chips should be dipped into the salt and then eaten). Sea salt from a grinder is treated like pepper, which is sprinkled or ground over the food. Mustard and other sauces also go on the edge of the plate. It is slightly insulting to your host or hostess if you season the food before even tasting it, so try a little first. If it is not to your taste, as people are using less salt nowadays, make a light comment, such as you have always liked very seasoned food, even though you know it is not good for you.

Table Napkins

These are sometimes referred to as serviettes. Fabric ones are best, and they should be put across the knee and not used as a bib.

Wine

If you are going to have only one type of wine, then it should complement the main course and not be served until then. Some people, however, like to have a glass with every course including the pudding, and to accompany the cheese with port. If you are not sure what to order, ask the waiter what he or she would recommend. You can judge a good restaurant on the quality of the house wine. This is a good option if you are not sure which wine to choose, and it is not a particularly special evening. It is not a good idea to choose the second-cheapest on the menu, because that is usually the one on which the restaurant makes the most profit!

If the event is important, visit the restaurant beforehand and talk to the wine waiter. When entertaining at home, go to a good wine merchant and ask for advice based on what you are planning to eat. The wine may cost a little more, but it will be well worth it. Again, give yourself time to try the wine. However well recommended it is, do not buy something you do not like.

Glasses

An array of glasses can sometimes be a puzzle. There should be as many glasses as the number of drinks you will be offered. The tallest and slimmest glasses hold champagne, if it is to be served; the next tallest, tulip-shaped glass is for white wine, and the largest is for red wine. The smaller glasses are for sherry (with soup) or port. Tumblers are for spirits or water. No wine glass should be filled more than two-thirds full, as it swamps the bouquet. One tip: if you know you are likely to be drinking very good wine avoid wearing strong perfume as it will mask the bouquet.

Sitting Down to Eat

When you are called to the table, either in a restaurant or a private house, do not linger to finish your drink or continue a fascinating conversation. The person who has been preparing the food will not be amused to see it spoil or go cold. If nobody makes a move, stand up and head gently for the door. For a formal meal, guests should not take their drinks with them (and it looks rude to gulp it down as if you are unsure whether or not you will get another), so leave what remains in the glass. During less formal evenings, your host will usually suggest you take the glass in with you. In a restaurant, a waiter will produce a tray to take drinks to the table.

Guests should wait to be seated by the host or hostess. If, however, they are told to sit where they like, it is usual to separate husbands and wives or partners, and for women and men to sit next to each other. Women sit first, but it is wise to wait a moment in case grace is said or any other ceremony observed. It used to be customary for the man to pull back the chair of the woman on his right, but as few do these days, you could be waiting all night!

At a formal dinner the hostess usually starts off by talking to the person on her right, so follow her lead. The most important man sits on his hostess's right, and the next most important on her left. The most important woman sits on the host's right, and the next on his left. This is also the case for single-sex business dinners.

Smoking

It goes without saying these days that you should ask if you can smoke. It is embarrassing for both you and your hosts if they have to ask you to stop. If you are absolutely desperate for a cigarette, make an excuse to leave the room, have a few quick drags and return as quickly as you can.

Tipping

I still find tipping of any kind uncomfortable. I wish people would either get a fair wage, or that service was automatically included, as is the case in many restaurants. Tipping is entirely personal, but here are some general guidelines.

Ten per cent of the bill is the usual tip given to waiters (this also applies to taxi drivers and hairdressers). You can, of course, give what you like, and many people do. If service is included in the bill, do not feel you should have to give more unless the service has been exceptional.

The receiver of the tip appreciates knowing that you are pleased with the service rendered. I have asked many men and women in various lines of work about tipping, and they all say that the size of tip is not important, nor do they feel particularly offended if they do not get one. Nevertheless, tipping is expected in many areas.

What if you are invited to stay in a grand country house where tipping has always been part of the culture? Colin McBain is the butler at Burghley House in Lincolnshire. Although the house employs only a fraction of the staff it did at the turn of the century, the amount of entertaining is considerable, especially during the Burghley Horse Trials. After a stay in a country house you would expect to leave the butler £10 to £15, the same for the cook and another £10 for the maid. If the under-butler or chauffeur has been particularly helpful, you would tip them too. Colin says he thinks nothing of it if people do not give anything; however, most do. Single ladies are not expected to leave a tip, but a single man is. In the case of couples, he tips the butler and other male servants while she sees to the female staff. You would leave the money in an envelope using the person's name, usually the Christian or first name.

Butlers and ladies' maids are very discreet, but their duties include unpacking for guests, so it is as well to bear that in mind! If you are shooting or fishing, you must also tip keepers, loaders and gillies. Ask your host for guidance as the amounts vary.

Complaints

If the service has not been good, then I will not leave a tip. Despite the emphasis on quality and customer care, there are still many places where the standards are not high, especially when the staff are young and the wages low.

It is important to say when you are not pleased with the way in which you have been treated, but you will get much further if you are courteous and well mannered. Having worked part-time in a hotel, I was surprised at the inconsiderate and often rude way I was treated. If you wish to complain to a waitress, you could try adapting the following examples:

'I am sorry, but the vegetables are cold. Do you think we could have some fresh ones?'

'I think this coffee has been sitting rather a long time. Would it be possible to have another cup?'

'We ordered some drinks a while ago now. Are they on their way?'

CORPORATE ENTERTAINING

Many companies still entertain their clients by inviting them to social, sporting and cultural events. While this should be great fun, do remember that you are there representing both yourself and your company, and therefore always 'on show'.

Flat Racing

This takes place in the summer. The most formal meetings are the Derby and Royal Ascot. If you are in the Royal Enclosure, a smart day dress and coat or summer suit is appropriate. Stockings and tights should be worn, and skirts must not be too short. Sundresses are to be avoided here too. Most people wear hats, but they are not obligatory. For Royal Ascot, a slip is usually sent with the vouchers mentioning points of etiquette. One to remember is that mobile phones are not allowed. The dress code is similar for other meetings such as Goodwood, but York and Chester, for example, are not so formal.

National Hunt Racing

The Grand National is the most famous meeting, followed by the Cheltenham Festival. As the weather is usually cold, a winter suit of fairly muted colours is most suitable with a warm coat and a hat. Many women like to wear a trilby. For a slightly more casual approach, jackets and skirts fit the bill. If you are not in a box, a Barbour or waxed jacket and warm trousers will be fine. Boots or stout shoes are also needed if the turf is soggy.

Point-to-Point

These are races run by horses that have hunted. As far as dress goes, they are much more casual affairs. A warm jacket with a skirt or trousers, green Hunter wellies and a Barbour will keep you warm and dry. A trilby or cap is also a good idea for extra warmth, as well as an umbrella because the season runs from the end of February to late April.

Shooting and Fishing

You are unlikely to be asked game shooting unless you have shot before. Most women accompany their husbands to enjoy a good lunch, unless they are keen to help beat. To tramp across the grouse moors you will need a warm shirt, a pullover, gloves and a tweed suit or warm trousers. Colours should be muted to help you blend into the undergrowth. Thick socks to go inside wellingtons or shooting boots and a Barbour complete the ensemble.

For a clay shoot, a Puffa or body warmer is worn over a jersey, thick skirt or trousers. Walking shoes or boots are required, and when the weather is cold, a hat or cap is advisable, as are shooting gloves.

Salmon fishing can mean wading waist deep into icy streams, so a pair of waders is a must! Warm trousers or jeans, a jersey, a Barbour, gloves and green wellies will be needed if the weather is very cold. Some kind of headgear is advisable both for warmth and safety. A fly in the head can be a nasty experience, even more so if it is in the eye, so glasses are often worn for extra protection.

Hunter wellies are priced around £50. Waxed jackets (of suitable strength and durability) cost between £80 and £100. Caps start at around £15, and sporting sweaters from £40. They are available at specialist gun shops and country sports shops.

Golf

If you are going to play golf seriously you need to be a member of a golf club and to buy proper equipment from specialist shops. When you are buying your clubs, you will be shown a wide range of clothes and shoes suitable for all seasons and at a range of prices. Most clubs do not allow jeans, shorts or T-shirts on the course or in the club house, so check with fellow guests before donning your Bermuda shorts, even in the hottest weather.

Tennis

If you are invited to Centre Court or Number One Court at Wimbledon, cameras are not allowed. For other tennis tournaments, it is worth checking with your hosts if you are unsure of the rules. The code of dress depends on the weather. A dress and jacket is the most versatile, as it is suitable for all weathers, but a summer suit that can be worn with a blouse underneath is also apt.

Henley Regatta

If you are invited to the Members' Enclosure, skirts must reach the knee. Otherwise, a summer suit or smart day dress is fine. Hats are optional.

Sailing

Hospitality sailing is usually a very social affair, and a trained crew is on hand to sail the boat. Most skippers are happy to show you the ropes if you fancy taking the helm, otherwise gin and tonics or hot rum are the order of the day.

For any sailing in this country, take warm trousers and sweaters as well as gloves and a waterproof jacket, as it can get very cold at sea. Rubber-soled shoes are essential so that you do not mark the deck. Deck shoes or wellingtons are suitable, depending on the weather. If you are staying somewhere overnight, you will need more formal clothes as well.

Glyndebourne Opera

This is a summer event, and most people take a picnic that is eaten in the gardens if the weather is at all clement. Men usually wear dinner jackets, so check with your hostess to see whether you should wear a short or long evening dress. It is as well to take an overcoat and an umbrella, as well as a rug to sit on.

TITLES

It is awkward to be introduced to someone with a title, whether it is a noble or professional one, and not know how to address the person correctly. To have the information at your fingertips will give you the confidence to cope with even the most grand occasion. However egalitarian we might be, people still value a title if they have one, and so it is only polite to use it correctly. Here are some guidelines (example names are given in brackets):

- The Queen is addressed as Your Majesty, and afterwards as Ma'am, which rhymes with lamb.
- The Duke of Edinburgh and The Prince of Wales are addressed as Your Royal Highness and then Sir.
- Other member of the royal family are addressed as Your Royal Highness and afterwards as Ma'am or Sir.

- Dukes and Duchesses – Your Grace.
- Marquess or Marquis – Your Lordship, My Lord or Lord (Cholmondeley).
- Marchioness – Your Ladyship or Lady (Cholmondeley).
- Earl, Viscount and Baron – Your Lordship, My Lord or Lord (Rochester).
- Their wives – Your Ladyship or Lady (Rochester).
- Baronet – Sir (George).
- His wife – My Lady, Your Ladyship or Lady (Carruthers).
- Baroness – Lady (Thatcher).
- Knight – Sir (Edward).
- His wife – Lady (Flynn).
- Dame – Dame (Judy).

Official Titles
- Ambassadors – Your Excellency, Mr Ambassador or Ambassador.
- Right Honourable Lord Mayors – My Lord Mayor or Lord Mayor.
- Lord Mayors – as above.
- Their wives – My Lady Mayoress or Lady Mayor.
- Mayors – Your Worship, Mr Mayor or Mayor (Higgins).
- Lord Provosts and Provosts – My Lord Provost, Provost, My Lord or Your Lordship.
- Aldermen and Councillors – Alderman (Jones), Councillor (Miller).

YOUR PUBLIC IMAGE ABROAD

It is useful to know something about other nations' habits in order to judge our own in a healthier fashion, and not imagine everything which differs from ours should be dismissed as ridiculous or illogical, as is frequently done by those who haven't seen anything.

Descartes

It is vital to find out as much as you can about the country you are about to visit. Chambers of Commerce or the Trade Associations and Embassies of those countries will have information and guidelines, and are usually very helpful.

Tack Training International runs a series of training courses in Business Culture Training to help people who are trading abroad or want to move into joint ventures with foreign partners. Gerald McGregor is a director of Tack

Training Worldwide. He explained to me: 'Cultures vary across nations and within nations. No culture is inherently superior or inferior, just different, and you need to be aware of these differences in order to be successful. Getting it wrong can lose you business.' A German politician once said on a visit to London: 'If I am selling to you I speak your language; if I am buying...dann müssen Sie Deutsch sprechen.'

Apart from learning the language of the country you propose to do business with, you must also master cultural differences in etiquette and manners. 'When you are at home you may argue about many things, and have widely differing views on both professional and personal matters, but you have many things in common,' says Gerald. 'But when you work overseas, or with people from different backgrounds, doing familiar jobs in unfamiliar circumstances can have a significant effect on the business itself.' Here are some examples:

- In Hong Kong, the buyer may not get to know you personally and meet you for lunch or dinner until there is a good business reason for doing so.
- In Japan, it is most impolite to sneeze or blow your nose in public (head for the nearest toilet).
- In Spain, you would not do a deal unless the client felt he or she knew you well enough to trust you.
- Southeast Asians judge a business person by their status and contacts.
- In the Netherlands, time is a commodity that is allocated to specific purposes. At the end of the working day, the Dutch switch off and private life begins.
- In the USA, the contract is what counts and the written word is all important.
- In many Middle Eastern cultures, business discussions blend naturally into personal conversation and family life. The spoken word is relied upon, and everything is renegotiable between friends.
- British managers working in the Gulf should learn something about Islam, as religion infuses every aspect of life out there.

The following points of etiquette might be helpful when doing business in Europe.

France
Meals
In France, meals may be rather lavish and expensive. Breakfast meetings are very popular, and can be held in a café, your hotel or the firm's dining room. A business lunch can take up to three hours, and business should not be discussed until the coffee stage. The days of habitually long lunches are over, however, and a quick brasserie lunch is the norm for day-to-day dealings. Whoever issues the invitation pays the bill.

Gifts
If you are invited to someone's home, flowers or good chocolates are ideal for the hostess, and malt whisky or Cognac for the host. Never take wine in France. Corporate gifts such as pens are fine, but anything too expensive could cause offence.

Dress
Clothes should be fairly smart and classic. The chic French are colour conscious: navy should be worn in the spring, and with white or red in the summer, but never in autumn or winter! Autumn and winter classic colours are grey, black, plum, beige and olive green. Tartan is always 'in' at the smartest occasions in late autumn.

Belgium
Meals
Lunch is the most likely form of business entertaining, and the person who has issued the invitation pays. If you are asked to someone's home, it is a real compliment. The Belgians entertain very lavishly, and if they take you out on the town, you will be treated to the best, which can take a long time as well as being expensive!

Gifts
Flowers are acceptable, but do not take alcohol. Modest corporate gifts are fine.

Dress
The Belgians dress rather conservatively. It is advisable not to wear trousers or very short skirts. Tights or stockings are worn in summer as well as winter.

Scandinavia

Although the guidelines below apply to Sweden, Norway, Denmark and Finland, there are cultural differences between these countries. When visiting a Scandinavian country, it is worth finding out as much as possible about its particular culture.

Meals

Breakfast meetings are popular, where the meal is substantial, but lunch hours are fairly short so you are most likely to be asked out for dinner. This could be at home or in a restaurant. If you eat at someone's house, it is important to phone and thank them the next day, (especially in Denmark).

Gifts

Flowers wrapped by the florist are popular, as are brandy or whisky. A company gift should be well made and stylish.

Dress

The Scandinavians take a slightly more casual approach than the British.

Italy

Meals

If you are invited to lunch or dinner, you should accept; otherwise you might risk seeming uncivil. The meal will be a long-drawn-out and expensive affair, and whoever issues the invitation usually pays. Let your host choose the restaurant, and bear in mind Italian time-keeping – do not make an appointment too soon after lunch!

Gifts

If you are invited to someone's home, take little presents for small children and flowers or chocolates. Corporate gifts should be of high quality and quite expensive.

Dress

Dress should be stylish and as expensive as you can afford, especially the shoes and handbag.

The Netherlands and Luxembourg

Meals

Breakfast meetings are not common, and lunch is unlikely to be a very ostentatious affair (perhaps even beer and a sandwich). Dinner is more relaxed, but not much business is discussed, as it is seen as a chance to get to know each other better. The person who issues the invitation pays. If you are invited to someone's home, it is a real compliment, so the hosts will appreciate a letter of thanks afterwards. Both these countries tend to be rather formal.

Gifts

Chocolates and flowers are acceptable gifts, but in the Netherlands they should cost at least £10 to £15. Wine can be agreeable in Luxembourg, but not in the Netherlands; if you are unsure, do not take it. From a company, the gift should be high quality but not too lavish.

Dress

Smart, conventional clothes are best. The Dutch are less formal, but trousers or short skirts are strictly for when you know people better.

Spain and Portugal

Although I have grouped these two countries together, there are strong cultural differences within Spain itself, as well as with its neighbour.

Meals

Breakfast meetings are not very common, lunches and dinners being the norm. Spanish lunches are likely to be pretty lavish, and you will be expected to drink wine with your meal. A business dinner will usually start at ten or eleven at night, but after a lunch that has finished at five, you will not be too hungry! Being asked to someone's home is a very encouraging sign, and you will probably eat a little earlier.

The Portuguese, on the other hand, will not take offence if you do not want wine at lunchtime. You are quite likely to be invited to someone's home, or even away for the weekend, so a letter of thanks never goes amiss.

Both these countries are very hospitable and will want to pay for you, so let them if they insist.

Gifts

In Portugal, take chocolates and flowers for the host and hostess (except red carnations which remind the Portuguese of the revolution). The Spanish expect corporate, but not personal, gifts, so do some research into the company to find out what is acceptable.

Dress

Women in Spain and Portugal do not as yet play such a significant part in business life, so dress should be smart and stylish but feminine.

Greeting Business Partners

The question of the embrace as a 'hello' can be tricky. Take your lead from your host or hostess, both in Britain and the rest of the world. Businesswomen in most countries kiss both cheeks these days, but the Dutch kiss three times and some Frenchmen do four! Although the Japanese shake hands, they prefer to bow and exchange business cards. In Japan it is important to know the rank of the person you are dealing with, so make sure you have a nice wallet with large number of impressive business cards with you! This goes for any business meetings.

afterword

Brains and talent are merely the entry fee for the race. To win, you have to know the secret: Do unto others as you would have them do unto you.
Burt Manning, Chairman of J. Walter Thompson

In this age of 'win at all costs' it is wise to remember that what goes around, comes around. Honesty and integrity are part of projecting a confident and competent impression. Creating the right image means dealing with people in a polite and courteous manner. Truly respecting others provides the basis for motivation, and nobody is more persuasive than a good listener. Creating the right image means preparing in advance for meetings, interviews, projects and presentations. It means dressing with thought and style.

I do hope this book has been useful in helping you decide what your image should be, and has gone some way towards helping you achieve it!

bibliography

Bradley, Dinah. *Hyperventilation Syndrome: a Handbook for Bad Breathers*,
    Kyle Cathie Ltd, 1994
Brandreth, Giles. *The Complete Public Speaker*, Sheldon Press.
Brandreth, Giles and Brown, Michele. *How to interview and be interviewed*,
    Sheldon Press, 1986
Bremner, Moyra. *Modern Etiquette*, Century Hutchinson Ltd., 1989
Carnegie, Dale and Ass. *The Leader In You*, Simon & Schuster, 1993
Gibbs, Paul. *Doing Business In The European Community*,
    Kogan Page Ltd., 1990
Hall, Nicola. *Principles of Reflexology*, Thorsons, 1996
Handley, Rima. *Homoeopathy for Women*, Thorsons, 1993
Hopkins, Cathy. *Principles of Aromatherapy*, Thorsons, 1996
Hill, Richard. *We Europeans*, Europublications, 1993
Leith, James. *Ironing John*, Doubleday, 1995
Lindenfield, Gael. *Self Esteem*, Thorsons, 1995
Lyle, Jane. *Understanding Body Language*, Hamlyn, 1989
Maitland, Ian. *Answer The Question; Get The Job!*, Century Business, 1993
Mather, Diana. *Surviving The Media*, Thorsons, 1995
McCarthy, Margot (ed.). *Neals Yard Book of Natural Therapies*, Thorsons, 1994
Spillane, Mary. *The Complete Style Guide*, Piatkus

Spillane, Mary. *Presenting Yourself*, Piatkus, 1993

Summers, Vivian. *Public Speaking*, Penguin, 1988

Tannen, Deborah. *Talking From Nine to Five*, Virago, 1995

Tannen, Deborah. *You Just Don' t Understand: Men and Women In Conversation*, Virago 1991

Velmans, Marianne and Litvinoff, Sarah. *Working Mother*, Corgi, 1993

index

Surviving the Media
How to appear successfully on TV, Radio or in the Press

Diana Mather

Whether appearing on Question Time, BBC Radio or simply an interview in a local newspaper, necessity calls for confidence and control. The message expressed must be clear and concise to avoid misunderstanding.

Diana Mather, an author who practises what she preaches, gives an insider's guide to the opportunities and pitfalls of promoting your 'cause' in the media.

There is now a bewildering variety of media, and each producer, each features editor, will be looking for new material. But what is expected? How can the chances of performing well under pressure be increased?

This book has the answers to these questions, and more:

- tackles the no. 1 fear – that of looking foolish
- what questions might be asked
- how to tailor messages to fit the audience
- what to wear
- problems and pitfalls

Working Well at Home
Managing the ups and downs of working where you live

Christine Ingham

Working at home is often the starting-point for many who become self-employed. However, problems can often arise out of working in the place where you live, including isolation, lack of motivation, conflicting demands and relationship problems. Left unresolved, they may affect the ultimate success or failure of the venture. Christine Ingham, herself a home-based worker, combines suggestions on how to manage both the personal and interpersonal difficulties with the recommendations of others who, between them, have over 50 years' experience of working at home.

Whether freelance, consultant, entrepreneur or just thinking about it, *Working Well at Home* is a personal and practical guide which can help. Home-based employees, including the growing number of teleworkers, will also find much of relevance here.

Coping with Change at Work

Susan Jones

It was not so long ago that our place of work provided us with a stable environment when other areas in our lives were in turmoil. This no longer is the case. Changes at work, whether technological, a promotion, a new job, a redundancy, a takeover or a new management style, can be highly stressful.

This practical guide aims to enable people to make sense of their new work situation and to excel. Checklists, step-by-step guidelines and real life case studies are included, making the book invaluable for those going through a period of transition. Other issues covered include self-esteem, status, control, management issues, career progression, risk and reward.

Intended primarily for people who are going through a period of change, whether at management or staff level, this guide is also helpful for anyone who wants to learn more about this topic.

How to Think on Your Feet

Marian K. Woodall

- have you ever been caught off guard in a meeting?
- stumped by a question during a sales call?
- suffered an embarrassing silence during an interview?
- thought of the perfect response – after the conversation?

You are responsible for one half of every conversation you have...in business, in community affairs, at home...and you must be able to respond appropriately and confidently in order to succeed. This book will teach you how to think – and speak – on your feet. The author, a top lecturer and seminar leader in business communications for 24 years, shares her experience with you and shows you how to:

- answer questions impressively – even if you don't know the answer
- buy time so that you can think before you speak
- retain composure when facing difficult questions
- polish your delivery skills

Everybody needs to be able to communicate well. Using proven theory, on-target strategies, and practical examples, Marian K. Woodall will help you improve *your* end of the conversation.

Coping with Stress at Work
How to stop worrying and start succeeding

Jacqueline M. Atkinson PhD

If you:

- work better to a deadline
- leave things to the last minute, then do them in a panic
- constantly feel in a rush
- feel full of dread at the thought of going to work
- often skip lunch
- stay late at the office, or take work home
- get tired, irritable and depressed

then you are suffering from stress. And if your way of dealing with it is to have another cup of coffee or reach for a cigarette, switch on the television or pour yourself a stiff drink you are making the problems worse.

This book offers original and varied ways of combating stress in the workplace. It will help you deal sensibly and practically with stress in a way that suits you and your working environment. You will discover your own stress triggers and look at resolving and easing stressful situations; you will learn how to relax, manage your time, and deal with problems before they deal you an ulcer.

How to Talk so People Listen

Sonya Hamlin

Have you ever come away from a meeting knowing that you haven't made your point effectively?

- have you ever made a presentation and felt audience attention slipping away?
- do you sometimes find it difficult to understand your business associates and meet them halfway?
- do high-powered encounters with the boss simply put you on the defensive?

If any of these problems sound familiar, then *How to Talk so People Listen* is full of the advice and help you need. You can identify what your listener wants from an encounter, and ensure that everyone gets the best possible results. Find out the best time to hold meetings – to lunch or not to lunch? – or how to gain prior knowledge of audiences and motivate them through self-interest.

This book exposes our preconceptions about communicating in the workplace and brings a new, highly effective dimension to this complex world. Sonya Hamlin is an Emmy-Award-winning chat show host and heads her own communications consultancy – she has acted as an adviser to the chief executive officers of such companies as American Express and Polaroid.

How to Think Like a Millionaire
Who better to teach you success than those who have made millions
themselves?

Charles-Albert Poissant

In this amazing book, which may be your first step on the road to millions,
Charles-Albert Poissant examines the factors that lead to success. He looks
at 10 of the world's richest self-made men, including Henry Ford, Paul Getty
and Stephen Spielberg, and demonstrates that their success was no accident
– they all shared certain principles and attitudes. Now you have the
opportunity to learn their secrets and use them for your own success.

From their experiences you can learn:

- the major prerequisites for becoming rich
- that age, education and lack of capital are irrelevant in attaining wealth
- the art of positive thought and positive action.

Mindstore
The ultimate mental fitness programme

Jack Black

Have you ever looked at people who are successful, either socially or professionally, and thought to yourself, 'How gifted', 'How lucky'?

Yet the truth is, 'How unlikely'. Either intentionally or subconsciously, successful people have developed a programme of mind-management which has enabled them to be different. This power is present in everyone, not just a 'gifted' few.

Jack Black, a leading motivational speaker and the founder of MindStore, has dedicated his life to discovering the techniques, beliefs, strategies and visions of success.

For the first time in book form, his message is now available to all. Entertaining, dynamic and above all easy to learn, discover for yourself how to:

- master emotions, finances and relationships
- let go of your 'I can't' philosophy
- gain renewed energy for life
- manage stress
- achieve your dreams.

SURVIVING THE MEDIA	0 7225 3010 2	£7.99	☐
WORKING WELL AT HOME	0 7225 3035 8	£6.99	☐
COPING WITH CHANGE AT WORK	0 7225 3130 3	£6.99	☐
HOW TO THINK ON YOUR FEET	0 7225 2963 5	£4.99	☐
COPING WITH STRESS AT WORK	0 7225 3095 1	£4.99	☐
HOW TO TALK SO PEOPLE LISTEN	0 7225 2958 9	£6.99	☐
HOW TO THINK LIKE A MILLIONAIRE	0 7225 3105 2	£6.99	☐
MINDSTORE	0 7225 2994 5	£6.99	☐

All these books are available from your local bookseller or can be ordered direct from the publishers.

To order direct just tick the titles you want and fill in the form below:

Name:

Address:

Postcode:

Send to Thorsons Mail Order, Dept 3, HarperCollins*Publishers*, Westerhill Road, Bishopbriggs, Glasgow G64 2QT.

Please enclose a cheque or postal order or your authority to debit your Visa/Access account —

Credit card no:

Expiry date:

Signature:

— up to the value of the cover price plus:

UK & BFPO: Add £1.00 for the first book and 25p for each additional book ordered.

Overseas orders including Eire: Please add £2.95 service charge. Books will be sent by surface mail but quotes for airmail dispatches will be given on request.

24-HOUR TELEPHONE ORDERING SERVICE FOR ACCESS/VISA CARDHOLDERS — TEL: 0141 772 2281